# OPPOSING VIEWPOINTS® SERIES

# Discrimination

# Other Books of Related Interest:

**Opposing Viewpoints Series**

Feminism

**At Issue Series**

Does Equality Exist in America?

Racial Profiling

**Current Controversies Series**

Homosexuality

# "Congress shall make no law . . . abridging the freedom of speech, or of the press."

*First Amendment to the U.S. Constitution*

The basic foundation of our democracy is the First Amendment guarantee of freedom of expression. The Opposing Viewpoints series is dedicated to the concept of this basic freedom and the idea that it is more important to practice it than to enshrine it.

# OPPOSING VIEWPOINTS® SERIES

# I Discrimination

*Jacqueline Langwith, Book Editor*

**GREENHAVEN PRESS**

*An imprint of Thomson Gale, a part of The Thomson Corporation*

THOMSON

GALE

Detroit • New York • San Francisco • New Haven, Conn. • Waterville, Maine • London

Christine Nasso, *Publisher*
Elizabeth Des Chenes, *Managing Editor*

© 2008 The Gale Group.

Star logo is a trademark and Gale and Greenhaven Press are registered trademarks used herein under license.

*For more information, contact:*
Greenhaven Press
27500 Drake Rd.
Farmington Hills, MI 48331-3535
Or you can visit our Internet site at http://www.gale.com

ISBN-13: 978-0-7377-3739-4 (harcover)
ISBN-10: 0-7377-3739-5 (hardcover)
ISBN-13: 978-0-7377-3740-0 (pbk.)
ISBN-10: 0-7377-3740-9 (pbk.)

Library of Congress Control Number: 2007933224

# Contents

## Chapter 3: Is Affirmative Action an Effective Remedy for Discrimination?

## Chapter 4: What Impact Does the Government Have on Discrimination in the U.S.?

# Why Consider Opposing Viewpoints?

> *"The only way in which a human being can make some approach to knowing the whole of a subject is by hearing what can be said about it by persons of every variety of opinion and studying all modes in which it can be looked at by every character of mind. No wise man ever acquired his wisdom in any mode but this."*
>
> John Stuart Mill

In our media-intensive culture it is not difficult to find differing opinions. Thousands of newspapers and magazines and dozens of radio and television talk shows resound with differing points of view. The difficulty lies in deciding which opinion to agree with and which "experts" seem the most credible. The more inundated we become with differing opinions and claims, the more essential it is to hone critical reading and thinking skills to evaluate these ideas. Opposing Viewpoints books address this problem directly by presenting stimulating debates that can be used to enhance and teach these skills. The varied opinions contained in each book examine many different aspects of a single issue. While examining these conveniently edited opposing views, readers can develop critical thinking skills such as the ability to compare and contrast authors' credibility, facts, argumentation styles, use of persuasive techniques, and other stylistic tools. In short, the Opposing Viewpoints series is an ideal way to attain the higher-level thinking and reading skills so essential in a culture of diverse and contradictory opinions.

In addition to providing a tool for critical thinking, Opposing Viewpoints books challenge readers to question their own strongly held opinions and assumptions. Most people form their opinions on the basis of upbringing, peer pressure, and personal, cultural, or professional bias. By reading carefully balanced opposing views, readers must directly confront new ideas as well as the opinions of those with whom they disagree. This is not to simplistically argue that everyone who reads opposing views will—or should—change his or her opinion. Instead, the series enhances readers' understanding of their own views by encouraging confrontation with opposing ideas. Careful examination of others' views can lead to the readers' understanding of the logical inconsistencies in their own opinions, perspective on why they hold an opinion, and the consideration of the possibility that their opinion requires further evaluation.

## Evaluating Other Opinions

To ensure that this type of examination occurs, Opposing Viewpoints books present all types of opinions. Prominent spokespeople on different sides of each issue as well as well-known professionals from many disciplines challenge the reader. An additional goal of the series is to provide a forum for other, less-known, or even unpopular viewpoints. The opinion of an ordinary person who has had to make the decision to cut off life support from a terminally ill relative, for example, may be just as valuable and provide just as much insight as a medical ethicist's professional opinion. The editors have two additional purposes in including these less-known views. One, the editors encourage readers to respect others' opinions—even when not enhanced by professional credibility. It is only by reading or listening to and objectively evaluating others' ideas that one can determine whether they are worthy of consideration. Two, the inclusion of such viewpoints encourages the important critical thinking skill of objectively evaluating an author's credentials and bias. This evaluation will illuminate an author's reasons for taking a particular stance on an issue and will aid in readers' evaluation of the author's ideas.

It is our hope that these books will give readers a deeper understanding of the issues debated and an appreciation of the complexity of even seemingly simple issues when good and honest people disagree. This awareness is particularly important in a democratic society such as ours in which people enter into public debate to determine the common good. Those with whom one disagrees should not be regarded as enemies but rather as people whose views deserve careful examination and may shed light on one's own.

Thomas Jefferson once said that "difference of opinion leads to inquiry, and inquiry to truth." Jefferson, a broadly educated man, argued that "if a nation expects to be ignorant and free . . . it expects what never was and never will be." As individuals and as a nation, it is imperative that we consider the opinions of others and examine them with skill and discernment. The Opposing Viewpoints series is intended to help readers achieve this goal.

*David L. Bender and Bruno Leone,*
*Founders*

# Introduction

"We were here before the mighty words of the Declaration of Independence were etched across the pages of history. Our forebears labored without wages. They made cotton 'king'. And yet out of a bottomless vitality, they continued to thrive and develop. If the cruelties of slavery could not stop us, the opposition we now face will surely fail. . . . Because the goal of America is freedom, abused and scorned tho' we may be, our destiny is tied up with America's destiny."

Martin Luther King Jr.,
"Letter from Birmingham Jail,"
April 16, 1963

"I would like to be known as a person who is concerned about freedom and equality and justice and prosperity for all people."

Rosa Parks, 1990

Discrimination may take many forms—gender discrimination, religious discrimination, sexual orientation discrimination—but its most notorious history in the United States is chronicled in the accounts of racial discrimination, particularly discrimination against African Americans. The history of racial discrimination in the United States is older than the country itself. Slavery of African Americans in the United States began even before the 1776 founding of the American republic and did not end until the Thirteenth Amendment to the U.S. Constitution was ratified in 1865. In

1838, U.S. soldiers removed about 17,000 Cherokee Indians from their lands in Georgia, Tennessee, North Carolina, and Alabama and forced them to relocate to Oklahoma and other western states. Thousands of Native Americans died during the relocation, prompting the route to be named the "Trail of Tears." During World War II, over 100,000 Japanese Americans living in California, Oregon, Washington, and Arizona were forced to leave their homes and possessions and live in government-run internment camps. In the early 1900s, most southern states enacted Jim Crow laws—named for a minstrel show character—requiring separate facilities for blacks and whites. There were innumerable laws requiring separate railroad cars, waiting rooms, bathrooms, restaurants, parks, beaches, schools, prisons, and many other "separate but equal" facilities.

During all of these events in U.S. history there were people who fought against discrimination: the abolitionist John Brown; Jeremiah F. Evarts, a leading opponent of Indian removal; and Mitsuye Endo, whose case against Japanese internment went all the way to the U.S. Supreme Court. In recent history, it is arguable that no two figures are more closely related to the fight against racial discrimination in the United States than Rosa Parks and Martin Luther King Jr.

Both Parks and King were a part of the African American civil rights movement, which began in 1954 when the U.S. Supreme Court ruled in *Brown v. Board of Education* that segregation in public schools was unconstitutional. The *Brown* decision was the first major blow against the Jim Crow system of racial segregation and the "separate but equal" doctrine. The civil rights movement led to the enactment of several important anti-discriminatory acts, such as the Civil Rights Act of 1964 that banned discrimination in employment practices and public accommodations, the Voting Rights Act of 1965 that restored voting rights, the Immigration and Nationality Services Act of 1965 that changed U.S. immigration policy, and the Civil Rights Act of 1968 that banned discrimination in the sale or rental of housing. The civil rights movement led by Parks and King helped to completely end Jim Crow laws and advanced the belief that all people are equal under the law.

Rosa Louise McCauley was born in Tuskegee, Alabama, on February 4, 1913. She grew up and went to school in Montgomery, Alabama. In 1932, she married Raymond Parks, a barber from Montgomery, who was a member of the National Association for the Advancement of Colored People (NAACP). Parks achieved two things that were very difficult for blacks at the time—particularly black women: She finished high school and she registered to vote. She did this in spite of the Jim Crow laws that made voting extremely difficult for blacks. In December 1943, Parks became active in the civil rights movement and joined her husband in the Montgomery chapter of the NAACP. The incident which made Rosa Parks famous and secured her spot in U.S. history came on December 1, 1955, in Montgomery. Taking the bus home from her job as a seamstress, Parks refused to give up her seat on the bus to a white man—as the Jim Crow laws required her to do. As Parks said, her only concern that day "was to get home after a hard day's work" and "the only tired I was, was tired of giving in." She did not give in and was arrested and fined for violating a city ordinance. Parks' courageous act of quiet defiance inspired African Americans and people everywhere, galvanizing the civil rights movement. In 1956, the U.S. Supreme Court struck down the Montgomery ordinance under which Rosa Parks had been arrested and outlawed racial segregation on public transportation. Parks moved to Detroit, Michigan, in 1957 and worked for U.S. Representative John Conyers. She died in 2005 at the age of 92. After her death, her casket was placed in the rotunda of the United States Capitol. She was the first woman to lie in state at the Capitol, an honor typically reserved only for U.S. presidents.

Michael (Martin) Luther King Jr. was born on January 15, 1929, in Atlanta, Georgia. King immersed himself in academics. He received a bachelor of arts from Morehouse College, and a bachelor of divinity from Crozer Theological Seminary, where he was elected senior president of a predominately white class. He received a doctorate of philosophy in Systematic Theology from Boston University and while there married Coretta Scott. After his studies, King became a church pastor at the Dexter Avenue Baptist Church in Montgomery, Alabama. Shortly, after Rosa Parks' act of defiance, Martin Luther King Jr. joined other black leaders and organized the Montgomery Bus Boycott, where blacks refused to ride Montgomery city buses. Under the leadership of King, the boycott lasted over a year (382 days) and brought worldwide attention to the American civil rights movement. The boycott also led to the emergence of King as a leader of the movement. King would go on to serve as president of a newly formed civil rights organization, the Southern Christian Leadership Conference, and to become a world leader in the fight against injustice and discrimination.

In 1963, *Time* magazine named King its "Man of the Year," saying: "Few can explain the extraordinary King mystique. Yet he has an indescribable capacity for empathy that is the touchstone of leadership. By deed and by preachment, he has stirred in his people a Christian forbearance that nourishes hope and smothers injustice."

King used the nonviolent techniques developed by the Indian nationalist and pacifist leader, Mohandas Gandhi (1869–1948) in King's fight against discrimination, leading protests and marches all over the country. Quoted in the *Time* article was Atlanta minister Ralph D. Abernathy, who said: "The people make Dr. King great. He articulates the longings, the hopes, the aspirations of his people in a most earnest and profound manner. He is a humble man, down to earth, honest. He has proved his commitment to Judaeo-Christian ideals. He seeks to save the nation and its soul, not just the Negro." King was granted the Nobel Peace Prize in 1964. Tragically, in 1968 he was assassinated in Memphis, Tennessee. His birth is commemorated each year in the United States on the third Monday in January, declared Martin Luther King Jr. Day.

The lives of Parks and King are intertwined and embedded in the history of racial discrimination in the United States. In *Opposing Viewpoints: Discrimination*, the contributors explore the many issues of discrimination in the following chapters: Does Discrimination Exist in the United States? How Does Discrimination Impact American Society? Is Affirmative Action an Effective Remedy for Discrimination? and What Impact Does the Government Have on Discrimination in the U.S.? The viewpoints presented on the following pages arise from the challenges of discrimination facing Americans in the twenty-first century. But they share a connection with past American struggles to acknowledge, to understand, and to remedy discrimination.

# Does Discrimination Exist in the United States?

# Chapter Preface

"Of course, it's illegal to discriminate—'genoism' it's called—but no one takes the laws seriously. If you refuse to disclose, they can always take a sample from a doorhandle ... or a handshake ... even the saliva off your application form." This is a quote from the 1997 science fiction movie *Gattaca*, in which genetically engineered humans are the elite in society and those whose genetic make up is determined naturally are called "invalids." The film may be science fiction but many people believe genetic discrimination poses a real threat to American society.

Genetic tests analyze a person's DNA to look for certain disease-causing genes. Tests have been developed for cystic fibrosis, Huntington's disease, sickle-cell disease, inherited breast cancer, and many others. The numbers of genes that can be detected by testing is constantly growing. As our scientific knowledge grows and technological advances are made, many scientists think it will only be a matter of time before there are genetic tests available for all human genetic diseases.

Genetic testing can reveal in advance the diseases that a person may face in the future. Many genetic diseases do not manifest until later in life. But the gene that causes the disease is present from birth. So genetic testing can predict diseases to which we are predisposed. A genetic profile contains very personal information about a person's future health.

Many people are worried that if employers or insurance companies obtain an individual's genetic profile, they may use that information to discriminate against the individual. For instance, an insurance company could decide not to offer health insurance or life insurance to a woman who carries one of the breast cancer genes. A potential employer may also feel that hiring the woman is too much of a risk. Scientists say that public fears of genetic discrimination are hampering their ability to recruit participants in genetic research and clinical trials of gene-based medicines.

As scientific knowledge advances and genetic tests become more routine, the prospect of genetic discrimination occurring in America worries many people. The contributors of the viewpoints in the following chapter discuss whether other types of discrimination exist in the United States.

*"Each day, African-Americans are confronted with hostilities from their fellow white citizens who see themselves as unofficial deputies."*

# Middle-Class Blacks Are Discriminated Against in the United States

*Ishmael Reed*

*In this viewpoint, Ishmael Reed contends that black men in the United States experience constant racial abuse from whites and particularly from the police. Reed chronicles several incidents of discrimination and harassment he—an educated, upper-class black man—has suffered at the hands of police. He suggests that racial injustices, discrimination, and the threat of police brutality permeate the existence of black men of any class. Reed is also contemptuous of American media and blames it for influencing the attitudes of whites against blacks. Reed is an American poet, essayist, and novelist.*

As you read, consider the following questions:

1. How old was Reed when he first experienced "organized hatred against African-Americans by the police"?

2. According to Reed, what percentage of crime in both cities and rural areas is committed by whites?

3. Who said, "[A]nd I experience, briefly, the secret fear of false arrest that every black male in America nurtures somewhere deep within"?

Three African-American writers, Patricia Williams, Lee Hubbard, and Cecil Brown, have complained about in taking younger relatives to see George Lucas's [*Star Wars* film] *The Phantom Menace* only to have these children exposed to stereotypical images of African-Americans. I'm glad that the children saw this movie in the company of these writers, who can prepare them for the combat they must wage in a society where media, including Hollywood, television, and the newspapers, present African-Americans as Faces of the Enemy, the typical portrait of African-Americans being similar to those found in a book entitled *Faces of the Enemy* by Sam Keen. This book dealt with propagandistic portraits of the Japanese, who, at that time, were engaged in hostilities against the United States. But the faces could well be those of African-Americans, who are often shown as inferior and simian and a threat to European women. A poster showing a Japanese soldier carrying a nude white woman over his shoulder is consistent with the images thrown up by the Bush family's Willie Horton campaign, which featured a black man who raped a white woman while on prison furlough. After this ad appeared, designed to link the rapist to [presidential] candidate Michael Dukakis, support for Bush among Southern white men rose 20 percent, according to Willie Brown, the mayor of San Francisco.

Each day, African-Americans are confronted with hostilities from their fellow white citizens who see themselves as unofficial deputies. I experienced an incident while working on this essay.

## Police Wage War Against Blacks

On July 6, I drove to the home of author Cecil Brown, who had had an encounter with the police at a swimming pool used by the University of California faculty. I had published a poem about the incident, "Strawberry Creek," in my zine, *Konch*. When this poem appeared in the local newspaper, the University of California police charged that Cecil Brown had been a menace to the women (white) bathers at the pool, although when Brown had asked the supervisor of the pool why the pool personnel had called the police, the supervisor couldn't give a reason. The police put out this story, I believe, because they wanted to cover their embarrassment at having harassed Brown, a Berkeley faculty member who had the temerity to use this pool, where one rarely sees a black person.

When I arrived at Brown's apartment at the Emeryville Watergate, I didn't find his name listed on the directory of the building where I usually met him for our walk around the Emeryville Marina, during which, from time to time, we are put under surveillance by the Emeryville police. I returned home to call Brown and he said he'd forgotten to tell me that he had moved to another apartment in the building and that he hadn't yet received a directory number.

We decided to meet in front of the building. During my first trip, I'd noticed a police car parked at the end of my block. When I left the block to meet Cecil, for the second time, the car followed me, changing lanes as I changed lanes and finally making a dramatic left turn after it was parallel to the left side of my car. I had been around longer than the children getting initiated into American racism by exposure to the propaganda arm of the occupation, Hollywood, and so I saw my encounter with the policeman as a skirmish. A strafing. Sort of like when an innocent passenger jet enters an unfriendly territory and is buzzed by fighter jets.

This policeman was a descendant of the white patrollers whom Booker T. Washington and others complained about.

The patrollers' job was to regulate the comings and goings of African slaves in the same way the UC-Berkeley police and the policeman on my block were regulating Cecil Brown and my comings and goings. The irony is that I have been the neighborhood block captain. As part of my job, I had complained to the police and to my councilperson about a pest house at a nearby intersection. It continues to be a safe haven for drug dealers and small-time criminals. . . .

Unlike the youngsters who accompanied the three intellectuals to see the Lucas movie, my first experience with organized hatred against African-Americans was not with Hollywood, but with the police. It occurred on Elm Street in Chattanooga, Tennessee. I was about three years old and the police were called out ostensibly to get rid of a pack of dogs that had been disturbing the neighborhood. We were told to remain inside. The police invaded the black neighborhood and began shooting up the place. It didn't occur to me at the time, and none of my relatives read anything into it, but now that I look back upon it, this was probably like war games. The police wanted to demonstrate their firepower to a neighborhood that might become troublesome. It was an act of intimidation. Most if not all of the riots that occurred during the sixties were the result of a police incident. These uprisings should be viewed as a stateside *intafada* [Arabic for "rebellion"]. . . .

Kofi Natambu, the poet and Malcolm X biographer, invited me down to the California Institute of Arts in April 1991 to give a lecture. We had left the Burbank airport and were walking in the parking lot when three plainclothes white men approached us. They identified themselves as members of the Airport Narcotics Security something or other. They wanted to know why I had used an exit different from the one used by the other Southwest passengers. I didn't have any baggage and so I used the main exit, while the passengers with bags used a different exit. The officers were very tense. On

Terry Gross's NPR show, *Fresh Air*, I had heard one of the many white experts of black things say that the police only hassled the black underclass. I thought of this when I identified myself as a professor at the University of California at Berkeley who was down for a lecture. They really lit into me then. They asked me to produce a ticket, which I did. I figured that if I exercised my rights and refused I would have been arrested and my briefcase planted with narcotics so that they could make a charge. Many whites believe that blacks are crazy when they accuse the police of planting evidence. These whites are the ones who are crazy, coddled by the criminal justice system and bewitched by the media into believing that American crime is black or brown when over 70 percent of arrests in both cities and rural areas are of whites. In fact, according to recent [as of 2003] FBI statistics, it is white adult crime that's on the increase. Many whites are programmed and manipulated by politicians who pay for intellectuals and op-eds written at the service of think tanks. They are seduced by an education that traffics in expensive lies. They live in an intellectually and culturally confined world that's similar to the one inhabited by the character in [the 1998 Jim Carrey film] *The Truman Show*.

At the turn of the century, Booker T. Washington complained that the media emphasized the "weaknesses" of African-Americans. According to Barry Glassner, things haven't changed. In his book, *The Culture of Fear*, Glassner criticizes the media for stigmatizing black men. "Thanks to the profuse coverage of violent crime on local TV news programs, night after night, black men rob, rape, loot, and pillage in the living room." The media does its part in influencing the attitudes of the white public, keeping white pathology a secret and serving as a sort of public relations annex for the police, so that warlike measures against the black people by the police are tolerated. The media have modern sophisticated tools that Joseph Goebbels would envy. . . .

## Black Middle Class Has Unique Burden

Though it may seem counterintuitive, racism might actually be more of a *unique* burden for the black middle class and affluent, than for the black poor. After all, African Americans at the bottom of the class structure face economic obstacles that are related to racism—especially historically—but which now also operate as part of the class system, with or without the presence of racial bias. On the other hand, black middle class and affluent professionals, who have largely navigated the class structure successfully, regularly find themselves—despite that success, or even *because of it*—wondering if perhaps they might be racially profiled or stereotyped, assumed to be a bad credit risk, a criminal, or less capable, despite mountains of evidence to the contrary.

Black professionals live with the knowledge that historically it has been precisely when persons like them began to "make it," that they were *most* vulnerable to attack. Lynching and mob violence by whites was often rooted in jealousy towards successful African Americans and black communities. The poor were "in their place" already, but the middle class and professional class of blacks were seen as having apparently forgotten theirs.

*Tim Wise, "The Oprah Effect,"* Black Agenda Report, *www.blackagendareport.com.*

## White Majority Aids War

The police wouldn't be able to wage war against the black population without the collusion of the majority of whites. In criticizing the growing prison industry that treats blacks as merchandise just as they were in slavery, Jerome G. Miller wrote in his book, *Search and Destroy:* "To the inner cities, all this criminal activity brought a war mentality, destructive strategies, and vicious tactics, which exacerbated the violence and fueled social disorganization far beyond whatever negative effects might hitherto have been attributed to single-parent homes, welfare dependency, or the putative loss of family values. The white majority embraced the draconian measures with enthusiasm, particularly as it became clear that they were falling heaviest on minorities in general, and on African-American males in particular." . . .

An indication of how little most whites care about how the blacks and browns are treated by the police comes from a poll about police brutality taken after an incident when a New York policeman sodomized a Haitian-American citizen with a toilet plunger. Most blacks and Hispanics felt that police brutality was a problem. Most whites didn't. (When NBC broadcast this poll, it left out the fact that Hispanics agreed with blacks—a way of isolating the black population as malcontents and paranoids who are devoted to political correctness.)

Randall Kennedy and other members of the Talented Tenth[1] might argue that African-Americans are under scrutiny because the crime rate among blacks is so high. But neither Kennedy nor Orlando Patterson, who also believes that the problems of millions of blacks are self-induced, can explain why other ethnic groups are targets of the police. In Northern California, an Asian-American was . . . shot to death by the police because, according to them, he was threatening them with martial arts moves. A Hispanic man, caught in the border wars now [in the early twenty-first century] being waged against Hispanics and Indians in the Southwest, described his ordeal, which resulted from being stopped by the border police, on Pacifica Radio News. He was stopped at 9 P.M. and when he told the officer that he was the town's former mayor, they said, "that don't cut no ice with us." It didn't cut no ice with them because they knew that in the eyes of the Anglo population, they had more power than a Hispanic mayor.

1. The educated top 10 percent of blacks, a concept introduced by black author W. E. B. Dubois.

On October, 22, 1998, the National Council of La Raza issued a news release complaining about police brutality aimed at Hispanics. "Groups ranging from Amnesty International to the Mexican American Bar Association to the Human Rights Watch have documented countless incidents of law enforcement abuse and excessive use of force. It is insulting, therefore to be told nothing is wrong when you have case after case [of] police officers not being charged and instead set loose back on the streets." Here again, the legion of writers who get paid by places like the *New York Times*, the *New Yorker*, the *New Republic*, and *Atlantic Monthly* to coast along on the familiar cliches about race and crime show their incompetence in analyzing such issues as police brutality. It's not single-parent households that get you into trouble with the law enforcement; Hispanics are often praised by the same writers for their strong family ties. It's your black or brown skin that marks you like the Star of David and the pink triangle marked Jews and gays in Nazi Germany. The Harvard Talented Tenth should get out of Cambridge [Massachusetts] from time to time and learn what's happening in this country.

Though the Harvard Talented Tenth believe that they have more in common with their upper-class colleagues than with other blacks, if the American government decided to exterminate blacks as they did the Indians, or to put them in concentration camps as they did the Japanese-Americans, or deport them as they did Mexican-Americans, the Tenth's white Harvard colleagues would sever ties with them. Wouldn't know them. Probably testify against them. Turn them in.

From the very beginning, when Africans were stored on ship prisons and were held in jail, innocent of any crime, while waiting to be sold, prison has been a second home for blacks and a home away from home. Even Clarence Thomas, a conservative, when watching a prison bus full of black prisoners said "there but for the grace of God go I," because he knows that he can be injured by a policeman for whom all

blacks are the same. Even Talcott, the right-wing black pro-
tagonist who wanders through the novel *The Emperor of Ocean
Park*, dismissing left-wing characters with terms like "pig-
headed" and who disdains P. C., fears a false arrest; he
said, ". . . and I experience, briefly, the secret fear of false arrest
that every black male in America nurtures somewhere deep
within." The powerful and the powerless. The police and their
enablers, the courts and the prosecutors, even put powerful
black politicians under surveillance. Maybe if the secret
government had spent as much time tracking al-Qaeda as it
did prying into the personal lives of black politicians and
leaders, the disasters of 9/11 could have been avoided. Recently the police detained the son of Detroit's mayor and a
few years ago, the son of Earl Graves, publisher of *Black Enterprise* magazine. In the late 1990s, some psychotic New Jersey
police held a famous African-American dancer to the ground,
until they saw that he was on the cover of that week's *Time*
magazine. . . .

## Hostility Now Taken in Stride

As I was winding up this essay, I had one of those encounters
that black men have to deal with too often. I went on an er-
rand to Oakland's downtown Civic Center. When I returned
to the garage to get my car, I got off on the wrong floor. I was
wandering about, trying to find my car, an activity that goes
on throughout the United States each day. A white woman
walked toward me. When she saw me she hesitated, a scene
that occurs throughout the United States each day when a
black man and a white woman are alone in a public space: I
ignored her and kept searching for my car. While walking
through one aisle, I noticed her at the other end of the garage.
She was staring across the garage at me. It was the kind of
stare of terror and hate that's gotten thousands of black men
incarcerated, maimed, or lynched and whole sections of the
Black Belts wiped out and their inhabitants massacred.

Pampered ex-suburban women, who saw their first black person when they joined the Student Nonviolent Coordinating Committee or moved into Greenwich Village, are saying that gender trumps race as the most serious social problem. The Talented Tenthers who, like their inspiration, W. E. B. DuBois, seldom leave a college campus, are saying that it's class.

But in an everyday situation like the parking garage, a white woman has more power than a black woman or a black male millionaire. When I came down another aisle, confused because I wasn't aware that I was on a different floor from the one where I had parked my car, I noticed a white man, whose job was apparently that of filling the cars on this floor with gas. He was standing, frozen, glaring at me. His fists were clenched. He had deputized himself as a patroller. He was ready.

Suddenly a security guard approached me and demanded that I produce a ticket. He had been watching me on video. (I guess they sent a Hispanic guard, so that if I were a really dangerous black man and I harmed him, it would be no big deal.) I told him that I had left it in the car. He said that it was probably upstairs. He escorted me upstairs and followed me until I located the car. Unlike those kids at the movie who were disturbed by the Phantom Menace, I took the incident in stride. I was a veteran and this was another day at the front.

*"I consider my life's experience a con-*
*clusive case against the idea that to be*
*black and middle class is to live with*
*white abuse as an everyday threat."*

# Middle-Class Blacks Are Not Discriminated Against in the United States

## John McWhorter

*In this viewpoint, John McWhorter claims that his life experiences do not support the notion that black men in America suffer constant racial injustices and discrimination. McWhorter says he is an average-looking black man, but he has never been discriminated against or harassed by the police. Sure, says McWhorter, he has experienced some racism. But it is an occasional event, something he shrugs off. It does not define his entire existence. McWhorter is a senior fellow at the Manhattan Institute think tank, a columnist for the* New York Sun, *and the author of several books.*

John McWhorter, "What About Black Middle-Class Rage?" in *Winning the Race*, New York: Gotham Books, 2006, pp. 199–205.

As you read, consider the following questions:

1. What event does McWhorter say moved him to step outside his linguist career to write on race?
2. What reason did some people provide to explain why McWhorter did not "harbor a deep-bone sense of constant abuse from whites"?
3. Did McWhorter experience discrimination in his academic career? Explain.

Although I try to argue on the basis of evidence from as many corners as I can find, I cannot even begin to claim that my writing on race is not founded, at heart, upon my personal experience. But because of this, I find [Ellis] Cose's book [*The Rage of a Privileged Class*] and other sources painting a similar picture of middle-class black experience, uniquely challenging to grapple with. This includes Ishmael Reed's views on race, founded upon a basic perception that even today, and even for middle-class blacks, every day is "Another Day at the Front," as he has titled one of his books. Deborah Mathis's *Yet a Stranger* and Lena Williams's *It's the Little Things* are similar examples, in which it is assumed that all middle-class blacks live lives in which snubs, glares, and open condescension from whites are routine. For Reed and Mathis, in particular, their assumption that all successful blacks experience incessant racist abuse naturally leads them to sharply condemn black writers who stray from the victim line—to them, this victimhood is indisputable, and thus the accusations of "sell out," and the like.

## My Life: No Constant Racial Injustices

The problem for me is that in my four decades as a middle-class black man in America, I simply have not experienced the endless procession of racist slights and barriers that Cose describes. The life I have led as a middle-class black person makes the "rage" of Cose's interviewees look, frankly, foreign and peculiar to me.

For example, Cose documents that after the Los Angeles riots in 1992, 78 percent of blacks in a poll agreed that "blacks cannot get justice in this country," and I well remember that line resonating among even comfortable, assimilated middle-class blacks at that time. I was aware of racial profiling—I grew up in Philadelphia where the naked racism of the police force under Mayor Frank Rizzo in the seventies was something even a kid couldn't miss hearing about regularly. I was even aware that if circumstances were just so, it was possible that I myself could have a nasty run-in with the police influenced by my color. Yet, I considered this an abstract and unlikely possibility, hardly tincturing my daily existence with a sense of imminent threat the way lynching did for all black men in the old South. And I presume that even Cose would not see this as the naïvete of a pampered soul, since he notes that "as awful as Rodney King's treatment may have been, most middle-class blacks know that they are not very likely to find themselves on the wrong side of a policeman's baton."

The nut was that I just couldn't see the King video as a symbol of my personal experience with white America, as "a glaring reminder that being black in America means that you operate under a different set of rules," as one of Cose's interviewees has it. In fact, the black response to the Los Angeles riots was the first of several race episodes in the nineties that frustrated me to the point that I was eventually moved to step outside of my linguist career to write on race.

Since then, one of the trickiest aspects of my second career is that I must work constructively with the fact that legions of middle-class blacks like me harbor a bone-deep sense of constant abuse from whites that I, to the best of my knowledge, have not experienced. Some have told me that this is because I am "clean-cut" but that is irrelevant; the idea is that these things happen to reserved, cultured blacks in expensive suits and cars, not just baggy-pants teens.

Nevertheless, here is my life.

# No Problems with Police

I have no problems with the police. I have never been pulled aside for a drug search or even touched by an officer. Actually, I have found it pretty easy to talk my way out of several moving violations, and the only time a police officer has stopped me for anything besides those was a black officer in Oakland who turned out to want to tell me how much he liked *Losing the Race!*

Only once do I recall ever being tailed in a store, and since so many blacks complain about this tailing, I have always watched for it. And my experience was that when I was about sixteen, a black friend and I dropped into a tiny Slavic bookstore in Philadelphia because I, as a language freak, was just intrigued by the place. The woman behind the register, a probably Polish-born middle-aged woman, was obviously terrified, and the store was so tiny that her displeasure was overwhelmingly present to us, to the point that we left the store. But that was not quite what most blacks complain of. After all, it was likely extremely rare that young black men entered that store, and what's more, it was just on the edge of a sketchy black neighborhood, such that we might suppose that the woman assumed that since aging books in Polish are rarely of interest to young black men (or most Americans), we might have been in there to rob her. I know I am supposed to simply decry her as "stereotyping" but I cannot. She was just human, reacting to a highly unexpected presence in a store located in a bad neighborhood, and as a foreigner from a country where blacks are virtually nonexistent, unlikely to be attuned to the factors of dress and demeanor distinguishing class among blacks.

Nor have I ever gotten the sense that a clerk considered me too poor to afford higher-end items—rather, I have the typical mainstream experience of having to ward clerks off from trying to get me to buy more expensive merchandise to up their commissions—that is, the same experience whites have. And despite my occasional television appearances, I have nothing approaching the public recognizability that would make such clerks think of me as a celebrity, and besides, I didn't have such experiences even long before I had ever been on television. No cashier has ever, to my recollection, asked me for an extra form of ID.

Not once has any white person questioned me to my face as to my credentials for engaging in an activity or profession. The barriers to promotion that many blacks report in corporate life and law firms have been unknown to me in academia. There, black faces are so "welcome" that on the contrary, being black often makes it easier rather than harder to get tenure. Possibly racist bias makes it harder to advance in some other fields, but definitely in linguistics during my experiences, being black has been nothing less than an advantage in employment and promotion. No whites in my earshot have said anything suggesting that they were "impressed" that I did something despite being black, despite Cose's interviewees regularly reporting such experiences. Indeed, I have occasionally felt that when I did a talk that was merely bread-and-butter, I got praise a little beyond what I deserved, and that this was definitely based in a quiet sense that it was great that I had been up there with my black face, showing that linguistics is an equal-opportunity realm. But I cannot see this as damning my existence or worthy of "rage," especially since I have never experienced this to a degree that could be considered outright condescension.

A Harvard Law School grad whom Cose interviews when she has advanced to a teaching position "feels ambushed whenever she hears a cutting racial remark," but my personal experience in almost two decades of life in academia gives me, in all sincerity, no idea what she is referring to. No one in academia has ever said anything like, "There goes that black stuff again" or "It's great to see a black person do a good job like you're doing" when I could hear it. I have recounted elsewhere that the one person who ever called me "nigger" was a drunken

## Not a Victim

Racism does exist today. I have been affected by it, but I am not its victim. My life is pretty good. I am far from wealthy. I still use public transportation to get back and forth to work. I am blessed through the Lord with a wonderful family, employment, a nice home (3 full bathrooms, 4 bedrooms, a family room, and a home office), and good health. Racism is blamed for a lot of things, but the straying away from Godly principles on family and personal responsibility are really the culprits in the black community. I have family members, friends, and co-workers whom agree with this, but continue to cling to racism as the main ailment of blacks today.

*Bev, aka Conserative Minority, my.opera.com, July 24, 2006.*

laborer reduced to mumbling it as I went back into my apartment after I had bested him in an argument, which I could only see as a desperate belch from a bested opponent whose life no one would envy and that mine had already soundly surpassed. I suppose I might also recall a little guy at a day camp when I was about nine who called me "blackey" once or twice, but in clumsy jest, and I am afraid that this experience in 1974 did not arouse in me any "rage," especially not of a sort that I would still harbor thirty years later.

I also feel it necessary to note that I consider my life's experience a conclusive case against the idea that to be black and middle class is to live with white abuse as an everyday threat. The nature of the issue is such that there is no survey necessary: I'm black, have been for a very long time, am not nearly light-skinned enough to look anything but, and these things simply do not happen to me. I am even told that I tend to look rather "serious" when walking down the street (I tend to be outlining and writing paragraphs in my head)—my default demeanor is not a smiley, gentle-looking one. Again, it doesn't matter that I don't look or talk "street" because the Cose idea is that the nastiness falls upon blacks of all "profiles." My life has taken place in Philadelphia, New York, Oakland, and San Francisco, all fertile breeding grounds for the Cose perspective. I also lived for years in Palo Alto, as a graduate student at Stanford, when I made extra money playing cocktail piano in wealthy white homes in surrounding towns. I therefore was often driving around those enclaves in a beat-up old car late at night—but was never once stopped as a suspicious figure (and officers could not have seen how "clean-cut" I was just seeing me through the car window, nor could they hear my tragically "proper" speaking voice). Also, I am a night owl and no stranger to bars; my favorite one in New York is in an area where late at night, "streety" young blacks congregate selling drugs and making a lot of noise. On countless nights I have made my way home from that bar in the wee hours, but never once have been bothered by an officer. If Ellis Cose had for some reason sought me out to fill out the anecdotes in his book, I would have come up with nothing to support the idea that white people bedevil me constantly with racist actions. This means something.

## I Am Not Alone

And I might also add that my life lends me my own "anecdotal" collection of "interviewees" who would concur with me. I know about eight black Americans—some friends, others long-term acquaintances—who readily agree with me that the middle-class black life of constant racist abuse that Cose and his friends depict is not theirs. No, they are not lower-class or blue-collar people; predictably, I tend to be closest to people with histories and lifestyles similar to my own. Nor, however, are any of them scions of the black elite, nor are most of them light-skinned, nor do all of them even have college degrees or significant bank accounts. But then, again, these things technically shouldn't even matter, as we are told that this abuse is aimed at any black person between about ten and sixty, regardless of demeanor, class, or accomplishment. And I can honestly attest that "whitey" just does not torment these people, or me, in the ways that Cose describes. *The Rage of a Privileged Class* got around quite a bit among reading blacks in the mid-nineties. I have no statistics to offer, but I have lost count of how many times I have asked middle-class black people, "Is what that book describes your experience?" and had them answer, "Well, no." Everybody has a story or two—or three. But "most of what life is"?

## Sure, Racism Happens Occasionally

However, as noted, it's not that my friends and I have not experienced racism. It's there indeed. For example, I know my racism when I see it and am not possessed of a fragile sort of pride that makes me reluctant to admit when racism has been imposed upon me (i.e., I have no quiet sense that racism is only something that should happen to, you know, *those* kinds of black people).

When I got my BA at Rutgers in the early eighties, a great many of the white students were products of lower-middle-class New Jersey families, their parents being products of pre–Civil Rights Act America. Even at that time, overt expressions of racism were taboo on campus, but it was impossible not to suspect that a lot of those kids did not have the most savory feelings about "the blacks." I recall a late-night debate with a white guy from Paterson, New Jersey, hardly a hotbed of racial progressiveness, in which it became clear that he considered blacks' overrepresentation in the ghetto to be due to their mental and even biological inferiority. I talked him into a logical corner in which he had to quietly but testily admit this in a word or two, and I just let the exchange stop there.

Or, I will never forget being at a deathlessly WASP [white Anglo-Saxon Protestant] wedding at an Oyster Bay country club, when the otherwise all-white male entourage and I retired to the bar. One of the club's members, not in the wedding, was a guy intoxicated like a cartoon character, staggering around approaching strangers and making lame, back-slapping jokes. As I started following the other men into the bar, he grabbed me and said, "I gotta let ya know—there're a lotta white women in there . . . HA, HA, HA, HA!!!!" But what did that mean? Clearly the fact that a nigger was going in there— and one better poised to attract said white women than he was—rattled him a bit. Ha, ha indeed—a little *Birth of a Nation* in 1995.

Or on women, back to Rutgers—a white woman I had become friends with told her white female roommate that she was enjoying hanging out with me, and the roommate interpreted her (mistakenly) as being interested in me romantically. My friend told me that the roommate said, "How could you? I could never be with a black guy." That was 1984, and the vignette resonates with Cose's depiction of a smiling white world roiling with subtle racist rot underneath, in that the roommate was always quite friendly toward me. She never knew that I was aware of what she had said (and I had better things to do with my time than confront her about it). The fact was that if I had by chance been inclined to try to date dear June (yes, that really was her name in all of its Cleaveresque resonance), I would have run up against a "No Coloreds" sign. Although, of course, she wouldn't have said so— leaving me unsure as to whether the problem was with me or something larger.

Another one was when I encountered something blacks often describe: an assumption that there is a potential romantic attraction between all black men and all black women, as if we do not have the same idiosyncratic issues of personal tastes and preferences that other people do. Some years back, Condoleezza Rice gave an address to the Manhattan Institute think tank. One attendee hinted to me in all seriousness that he hoped that I would have the occasion to talk to Ms. Rice while she was visiting since *she and I would make a good couple*. I see: the National Security Advisor to the President of the United States, a richly accomplished figure on the world stage, slips her phone number to a slightly prominent linguist and writer a decade-plus younger than she whom she has likely never heard of until that night. The Elephant Man I am not, but I am also no Denzel, and so one would not expect me to pull this off by brunt of sheer hottitude. And make Rice and me white equivalents of our respective selves and no one would ever even begin to imagine such a thing: Imagine, say, an unmarried Diane Sawyer and even a writer light-years more prominent than me such as Jonathan Franzen. The idea was based on a sense that for Rice and me, blackness alone is so overwhelmingly definitive that a romantic attachment would be immediately imaginable even between people so vastly different in terms of place in the world, past experience, and even age. That is, there is a sense here that blacks are a different species: *Homo niger*, perhaps.

## I Don't Feel It

So, yes, things happen, and those are far from the only cases I could recount. But when a retired black psychologist intones to interviewers that "We live lives of quiet desperation generated by a litany of *daily* large and small events that whether or not by design, remind us of our 'place' in American society," I'm sorry, but I just don't feel it. For me, these things have been occasional episodes, extraordinary happenings, rather like, say, getting caught in a brief hailstorm—something a little odd and a little annoying that happens every once in a while. Hail does not set the tone of a lifetime.

> "Current rulings in employment law have permitted employers to hide behind the 'she-didn't-ask-for-more' and other so-called market-based excuses as legitimate reasons for paying women less than men for the same job."

# The Wage Gap for Women

## Debra Katz and Justine F. Andronici

*In the following viewpoint, Katz and Andronici argue that employers use several excuses for paying women less than men, one of which is that women fail to negotiate their salaries. Women who do try to negotiate their salaries, the authors argue, are often penalized because they appear pushy and aggressive and do not fit their gender stereotype. Katz and Andronici claim that it is hard to prove gender-based pay discrimination under U.S. antidiscrimination and equal pay laws because these laws fail to account for gender differences in salary negotiations. Katz and Andronici are attorneys specializing in women's rights issues.*

As you read, consider the following questions:

1. Under the federal antidiscrimination law, what must women prove in order to hold employers liable for pay discrimination?

2. In a study at Carnegie Mellon University, what percentage of first time job-seeking women negotiated their salaries? What percentage of men negotiated their salaries?

3. According to the U.S. Supreme Court in the 1989 *Price Waterhouse v. Hopkins* case, who should bear the responsibility for preventing gender-based stereotypes that harm women?

Imagine you're a woman interviewing for a job you really want. You get a call the next day with an offer, and immediately accept it. Later, though, you discover that a male counterpart earns significantly more than you. When pressed for an explanation, your boss tells you that the man demanded more when he negotiated his starting pay.

## Proving Wage Discrimination Is Difficult

If you sue for wage discrimination under this scenario, your chances of success would, unfortunately, be slim. Current rulings in employment law have permitted employers to hide behind the "she-didn't-ask-for-more" and other so-called market-based excuses as legitimate reasons for paying women less than men for the same job or one of equivalent value.

Here's how the system has been working: Under the crucial federal antidiscrimination law—Title VII of the Civil Rights Act of 1964—a woman must prove that an employer was motivated by intent to discriminate when deciding to pay her less than a male counterpart. Therefore, employers who merely take advantage of the fact that a woman is willing to work for less won't be held liable for pay discrimination.

In a slightly different vein, under the federal Equal Pay Act—which requires only that an employee prove that an employer paid men and women differently even though they performed the same job, not an intent to discriminate—the law lets employers escape liability if they can show that the pay

## Women of All Races Earn Less than Their Male Counterparts

White men are not the only group that out-earns women, although the wage gap is largest between white men and white women. Within other groups, such as African Americans, Latinos, and Asian/Pacific Islanders, men earn more than women (Source: U.S. Census Bureau).

*Hilary M. Lips, "The Gender Wage Gap:*
*Debunking the Rationalizations," www.womensmedia.com.*

differentials are caused by a "factor other than sex." To avoid legal liability, employers trot out market-based excuses: The woman asked for less money, did not seek or negotiate strongly for a raise, or came to the job from a position that paid less. These excuses have, for example, shielded universities that paid female coaches considerably less than male coaches, or compensated female faculty members in male-dominated disciplines less than their male colleagues.

## Salary Negotiation Gender Differences

The current legal standard fails to account for the insidious results of gender differences in salary negotiation. A study of master's-degree candidates at Carnegie Mellon University by economist Linda Babcock found that only 7 percent of first-job-seeking women negotiated their salary, as opposed to 57 percent of men. There was no small consequence to this failure to negotiate. In their book *Women Don't Ask: Negotiation and the Gender Divide* Babcock and co-author Sara Laschever found that candidates who negotiated increased their starting salaries by 7.4 percent (about $4,000), and that the starting salaries of males averaged 7.6 percent higher than the females'.

Babcock calculated that failing to negotiate for a first salary can lead to an overall loss of over $560,000 by age 60. That comprises a good chunk of the estimated overall wage gap between men and women—further exacerbated by such other forms of gender discrimination as mommy tracking and sexual harassment—which Brandeis University Women's Studies Research Center resident scholar Evelyn Murphy projects (using U.S. Census figures) costs women between $700,000 and $2 million over the course of a career.

## Women Trained Not to Negotiate

But aren't women at fault for not negotiating? Babcock concluded that women are essentially trained not to and penalized by employers when they do. Rigid gender-based stereotypes and behavioral norms urge women to behave modestly and wait to be given what they deserve rather than negotiate for it. The economist also has shown that negotiating can sometimes hurt a female job candidate. In research she co-published last year [2005], she found that female candidates who ask for higher salaries before receiving a formal job offer are often not hired at all. Not surprisingly, males who negotiate do not face similar negative consequences. This empirical evidence supports what many women already know from experience: When they ask for what they deserve, employers often view them as overly aggressive, pushy or too "difficult" to hire.

Given the tremendous ramifications of this pervasive discrimination, it's high time for courts to stop accepting excuses based on women's failure to negotiate, and instead put the burden of pay discrimination where it belongs: on employers. It's the employers who should be obligated to carefully evaluate their pay structures to ensure that female applicants are paid what the position is worth—and what similarly situated male applicants would be paid.

This sort of legal approach is not unprecedented. The U.S. Supreme Court has been willing to crack down on the use of stereotypes when they operate to the detriment of women. In the landmark 1989 case *Price Waterhouse v. Hopkins*, for example, the Court held that the employer should bear the responsibility for preventing the application of harmful gender-based stereotypes that disadvantage women.

## Women in a Catch-22

Ann Hopkins, a certified public accountant who was seeking promotion to partner in her firm, was criticized by male partners for not fitting traditional gender roles and was turned down despite her exemplary record. She was deemed too "macho" by one partner, and in need of "a course at charm school" by another. The Court concluded that the employer should be held accountable for letting these stereotypes pollute the promotion decisions, noting, "An employer who objects to aggressiveness in women but whose positions require this trait places women in an intolerable and impermissible Catch-22: out of a job if they behave aggressively and out of a job if they do not. Title VII lifts women out of this bind."

Women are in a similar bind when it comes to negotiating for equitable pay. Employers should not let outdated gender norms taint their employment decisions. And it's time for advocates to push the courts to step in and tell employers: no more excuses for gender-based pay discrimination.

"The widely propagated myth of miserably unhappy women victimized by widespread discrimination is unfounded. Women actually report higher levels of job satisfaction than do men, despite our lower average earnings."

# Wage Discrimination Against Women Does Not Exist

*April Kelly-Woessner*

*In this viewpoint, April Kelly-Woessner contends that women do not get paid less than men because they are discriminated against. Instead, women make less money than men because they choose different careers and have different priorities when they select jobs. Women's priorities include things other than compensation, such as emotional rewards and healthy work environments. Kelly-Woessner says women have higher levels of job satisfaction, despite their lower wages. Kelly-Woessner is an assistant professor of political science at Elizabethtown College.*

April Kelly-Woessner, "The Wage Discrimination Myth," *The American Enterprise Online*, June 2005. www.taemag.com. Reproduced with permission of *The American Enterprise*, a national magazine of politics, business, and culture.

As you read, consider the following questions:

1. According to Kelly-Woessner, the statistic that "women make 76 cents to the dollar for the same work as men" is what kind of statistic? Explain.
2. Men are how many times more likely than women to suffer a fatal injury on the job?
3. According to Kelly-Woessner, how do women's organizations define success?

On the first day of class, I ask students in my "Women and Politics" course at Elizabethtown College to write a brief statement about the status of women in America. The majority of students cite the same statistic to support a claim that women are disadvantaged: Women make 76 cents to the dollar for the same work as men.

## Distorted Facts

Though many students believe this to be a fact, it is actually what statisticians refer to as a mutant statistic, one so distorted and misinterpreted that its current incarnation is a blatant falsehood. This falsehood has been perpetuated by the media, politicians, and academics for many reasons, most of them political. It is used as a call to arms, as in the recent rash of television and billboard advertisements that littered Pennsylvania, courtesy of the Pennsylvania Commission for Women. In what the commission refers to as a "shocktoid campaign," they make the claim that women are paid 23 percent less for doing the same job as a man.

This is a gross and irresponsible distortion of the facts. It is true that women in Pennsylvania who work full time make 23 percent less than men in Pennsylvania who work full time. This "wage gap" does not, however, occur where men and women work at the same job. Rather, women make 23 percent less than men largely because they work in different ways, in different fields.

## Unequal Doesn't Always Mean Unfair

When it comes to pay discrimination, the one statistic you hear over and over is that women make only 76 cents for every dollar a man earns.

To the average person, that ratio gives the false impression that any woman working is at risk of being paid 24 cents less per dollar than a man in the same position.

But all the wage-gap ratio reflects is a comparison of the median earnings of all working women and men who log at least 35 hours a week on the job, any job. That's it.

It doesn't compare those with equal work, equal training, equal education or equal tenure. Nor does it take into account the hours of overtime worked.

The wage gap, in short, "is a good measure of inequality, not necessarily a measure of discrimination," said Heidi Hartmann, president of the Institute for Women's Policy Research.

Unequal doesn't always mean unfair. Much depends on the reasons for disparity. And, Hartmann notes, "parsing out (the reasons for the gap) is difficult to do."

Factors may include: more women choose lower-paying professions than men; they move in and out of the workforce more frequently; and they work fewer paid hours on average.

*Jeanne Sahadi, "The 76-cent Myth,"*
*CNNMoney.com, February 21, 2006.*

The mutant version of the statistic suggests that employers are blatantly discriminating against women. But what if the truth is that men and women make very different career choices? In that case, no amount of anti-discrimination legislation will change the facts.

# Different Career Choices

It is undeniable that women and men are often interested in different occupations. The majority of social work and elementary education majors in college are women. Men still dominate the sciences. While it may be true that society has historically undervalued the fields that women enter simply because they were women's fields, this historic discrimination fails to explain why similarly skilled males and females continue to choose different fields today. If their only consideration were income potential, surely women would flock to the highest paying fields. I have many female students who are clearly capable of doing well in male-dominated fields like math and science; yet they choose to focus their studies elsewhere. Perhaps they know something that equal pay advocates do not: that we cannot measure happiness and success purely in monetary terms.

Also bear in mind that, in a free market economy, we must offer high wages to attract people to less desirable jobs. Some of the jobs traditionally held by men pay more because they are dangerous or odious. According to the Bureau of Labor Statistics, there were 5,559 fatal workplace injuries in 2003—of these, 5,115 were men and 444 women. Adjusted for the slightly higher number of men in the labor force, men are more than ten times likelier to suffer a fatal injury on the job than are women. Is it unreasonable to expect that employers would have to dish out higher salaries to get workers to fill dangerous positions? Should we encourage women to pursue more hazardous work?

When researchers compare men's and women's wages for the same occupation, the gender gap is reduced. But even these studies do not account for differences between men and women in things like hours worked. They compare average weekly salaries for all "full time" wage earners, whether they work 40 hours per week or 70. Yet Gallup polls show that men are twice as likely as women to put in overtime of 50 hours a week or more.

## Different Priorities

Suppose we could compare men's and women's wages for the same occupation while controlling for hours worked and job seniority. Even then it would be a leap to assume that any remaining difference is due to discrimination against women. Based on survey research findings, we know that women and men have different priorities when it comes to selecting a job. Men place more weight on compensation and potential for advancement, while women favor instead an emotionally rewarding job and healthy work environment.

My husband and I are perfect illustrations of these self-selecting priorities at work. We have the exact same degree from the same university. We are both assistant professors of political science. He makes quite a bit more money than I do. Why? Because I chose a position at a small teaching college that pays less, while he chose a large research institution that pays more. I like my job better and would not want to trade it for his. I actually turned down interviews at universities that would have paid me more. Yet someone who merely compared our job titles, credentials, and salaries would be tempted to conclude that I am the victim of gender discrimination. I assure you I am not.

We are all so familiar with the story told by those who profess to speak for women. Women are disadvantaged. Women are unhappy. It is men's fault. The problem is that the evidence no longer supports these claims, especially in the workforce. While there are certainly isolated instances of gender discrimination, the widely propagated myth of miserably unhappy women victimized by widespread discrimination is unfounded. Women actually report higher levels of job satisfaction than do men, despite our lower average earnings.

Yet women's organizations insist on defining success and happiness purely in economic terms. So of course when they discover that wages are not equal, they cry sexism, never considering the possibility that the gap is due to women's choices. Their story is tired. Their political agenda is disconnected from reality.

"Gay and lesbian rights are not 'special rights' in any way. It isn't 'special' to be free from discrimination—it is an ordinary, universal entitlement of citizenship."

# Opposing Same-Sex Marriage Discriminates Against Gays

### Julian Bond

*In the following viewpoint, Julian Bond—accepting an award from the National Gay and Lesbian Task Force—asserts that prohibitions on same-sex marriage are discriminatory. Gay rights are civil rights, says Bond, and all Americans should have the right to marry the person of their choice, whatever their sexual orientation. Bond draws comparisons between the fight for gay and lesbian rights and the African-American civil rights movement, saying sexuality, like race, is a condition people are born with and cannot change. As of 2007, Bond is the chairman of the National Association for the Advancement of Colored People (NAACP).*

As you read, consider the following questions:

1. Which state supreme court was the first to strike down laws prohibiting interracial marriage?

Julian Bond, "Address at the National Gay and Lesbian Task Force's 10th Annual Miami Recognition Dinner," National Gay and Lesbian Task Force, November 4, 2006. Reproduced by permission.

2. What reason does Bond give for the statistic that black same-sex couples are more likely than white same-sex couples to hold public sector jobs?

3. Bond mentions that he and others who worked in the African-American civil rights movement were uplifted by a radio address. Who gave the radio address and when?

I am more than honored to receive this award, and want to express my thanks to all responsible for it. I want to promise you that I will intend to live my life as if I actually deserve it. I believe it represents a common acknowledgement that denial of rights to anyone is wrong and that struggles for rights are indivisible.

I feel tonight a little like the great abolitionist Frederick Douglass must have felt in April, 1888. Douglass, by then an old man, was addressing a women's convention in Seneca Falls, New York. They praised him for his devotion to the cause of women's suffrage. Forty years earlier, at the world's first Women's Rights Convention, when Susan B. Anthony made a motion that American women had the right to vote, it was Douglass who seconded the motion.

In 1888, Douglass reflected back on that moment and told his audience,

> When I ran away from slavery, it was for myself; when I advocated emancipation, it was for my people; but when I stood up for the rights of women, self was out of the question, and I found a little nobility in the act.

You have all made me feel noble tonight.

I am proud to represent an organization that has fought for justice for nearly 100 years, and while we've won many victories, we know—you know—there are other battles yet to be waged and won.

# So-Called Marriage Amendments Are Wrong

At the NAACP we stand in opposition to the Federal Marriage Amendment and its wrong-headed versions in several states.

The NAACP recently passed a resolution to strengthen families, including yours. We promised to "pursue all legal and constitutional means to support non-discriminatory policies and practices against persons based on race, gender, sexual orientation, nationality or cultural background."

We know there was a time, not so long ago, when black people in this country couldn't marry the person of their choice either. The California Supreme Court was the first, in 1948, to strike down laws prohibiting interracial marriage.

More recently, the California legislature became the first to legalize gay marriage. Will New Jersey be next?

As California goes, so goes the nation. It's just a matter of time.

Almost twenty years after California legalized interracial marriage, the United States Supreme Court heard the aptly named case *Loving v. Virginia.*

A married couple—Richard Loving, a white man, and Mildred Jeter, a black woman—won a ruling from the Court that Virginia's miscegenation laws were unconstitutional. That case enabled me to get married in Virginia. That case recognized marriage as one of the inviolable personal rights pursuant to happiness.

Now, Virginia is one of eight states this election season with a so-called "marriage" constitutional amendment on its November 7th [2006] ballot. Voters there and in Arizona, Colorado, Idaho, South Carolina, South Dakota, Tennessee and Wisconsin will be asked to exclude some people in their states from the law's protection. Twenty other states already have added such amendments to their constitutions.

While the ostensible purpose of these amendments is to enshrine in state constitutions additional—and unneeded—prohibitions against same-sex marriage, in fact they have several different purposes—all of them are anti-marriage, all of them wrong-headed, all of them discriminatory, and all of them politically based. One writer says, "Conservative preachers and right-wing activists can't let go of gay marriage. They're still using its 'threat' to traditional families to rally their parishioners, lest they forget to be judgmental and willingly slip into love and mercy."

Marriage in the United States today has a 50 percent failure rate. I should think we would welcome anyone who wanted to support and join this failing institution. Why are we afraid of those who want their loving relationships to have the same benefits of the law's protections as others have had since the country was founded?

President Bush has said marriage is "the most fundamental institution of our civilization." Isn't that precisely why we should support, not oppose, gay marriage? Many of the state-level Constitutional amendments, like the one proposed in Virginia, do more than ban same-sex marriage; they also ban civil unions and important protections for male/female domestic partnerships.

Proponents of these amendments argue they are insurance against so-called "activist" judges, presumably like those on the Supreme Court whose activism interfered in the 2000 election process and crowned George W. Bush as President.

The real purpose of these amendments is to draw conservative voters to the polls, offering them the red meat that motivates so many Americans to cast votes.

But in a survey of pastors reported in the December 2004 issue of *Facts and Trends* magazine, when pastors were asked to name the number one threat to family, 43% named divorce, 38% named negative influences in the media, 36% cited materialism, 24% said absentee fathers, families without a stay-at-home parent were listed by 18%, pornography was a reason for 17%, morality not being taught in schools was mentioned by 14%, and poverty, unemployment and a poor economy were mentioned by 13%.

Same-sex marriage did not make the list.

## Marriage Is a Civil Right, Not a Religious Right

We know there are many who base their support of these laws and their opposition to same-sex marriage on Biblical inerrancy, on the proposition that Leviticus 18:22 prohibits homosexuality and God's law must be obeyed. Believers ought not force their laws on people of different faiths or people of no faith at all. Marriage is a civil right. If you don't want gay people to marry in your church, all right. But you cannot say they can't be married in city hall because of your religious beliefs.

Most public officials place their hands on the Bible and swear to uphold the Constitution. They don't put their hands on the Constitution and swear to uphold the Bible.

Religious extremists want to install a Christian caliphate in America by replacing laws made by men with laws made by religion. They are cafeteria Christians, picking a Bible injunction from column A while ignoring those from columns B through Z.

But I cannot imagine even the most fervent Christian obeying all of God's laws, and I hope we never see all of those laws applied. . . .

## Homophobia Weakens Our Nation

The Bible's Ten Commandments are an exceptional guide for us all—but strict literalism calls upon us to adopt behaviors most would shun and cast aside.

Rampant homophobia is dangerous to our national security. The United States military spent more than $200 million

## Gay Marriage Around the World

Gays all over the world are fighting for equal protection under the law, including legal gay marriage. Some may think granting civil, registered or domestic partnerships is enough—seeking to preserve the legal definition of marriage as between a man and a woman. Most civil, domestic and registered partnership laws around the world provide fewer benefits than full marriage. So in many cases, life-long partners are denied some or all of the rights of marriage simply based on their sexual orientation.

Nations that recognize gay marriage:

*Canada*: in June of 2005, the Canadian Parliament enacted a law allowing legal marriage for same-sex couples.

*Belgium*: the second nation to legalize same-sex marriage in 2003.

*Netherlands*: the first country to grant gay marriage in 2001.

*South Africa*: . . . the fifth nation to recognize gay marriage in 2005. . . .

U.S. states that recognize gay marriage:

*New Jersey*: On October 25, 2006, the New Jersey Supreme Court ruled that New Jersey must allow same-sex couples to marry. However, the court left the decision up to lawmakers whether those rights would be extended in the form of full marriage or civil unions that allow gay couples all of the privileges of marriage. . . .

*Massachusetts*: On May 17, 2004 Massachusetts became the first U.S. state to legalize same-sex marriage.

*Ramone Johnson, "Gay Marriage Around the World,"*
*About.com. gaylife.about.com.*

to recruit and train personnel to replace the 10,000 troops discharged for being openly gay between 1993 and 2003. Last year, they discharged twenty Arab-speaking personnel whose skills were vital to the war on terror.

Homophobia weakens our national defense. In 1989, a Pentagon study concluded sexuality "is unrelated to job performance in the same way as is being left-handed or right-handed." Our fighting women and men, gay and straight, have fought in Iraq beside troops from Australia, Britain, Italy and Spain—all countries that permit gays to serve openly.

There are more than a million children being raised today in America by gay and lesbian parents—all of them disadvantaged by the inability of their parents to have the benefits and legal protections that marriage affords.

Black same-sex couples are more likely than white same-sex couples to hold public sector jobs, probably because these jobs often provide domestic partner benefits like health insurance, benefits threatened by Virginia's proposed amendment. And black same-sex couples are as likely as opposite-sex couples to report having lived in the same residence as five years earlier, an indication of the stability of their relationships.

Supporters of opposite-sex marriage say that it must remain sacred in order to encourage childbearing and to ensure the future of the human race. But there's not a couple married anywhere, now or at any time in the past, who was asked if they would have children to prove they could procreate before their marriage license was issued.

When I am asked, "Are gay rights civil rights?" my answer is always, "Of course they are."

Civil rights are positive legal prerogatives—the right to equal treatment before the law. These rights are shared by all. There is no one in the United States who does not—or should not—share in these rights.

Gay and lesbian rights are not "special rights" in any way. It isn't "special" to be free from discrimination—it is an ordinary, universal entitlement of citizenship. The right not to be discriminated against is a commonplace claim we all expect to enjoy under our laws and our founding document, the Constitution. That many had to struggle to gain these rights makes them precious—it does not make them special, and it does not reserve them only for me or restrict them from others.

When others gain these rights, my rights are not reduced in any way. The fight for "civil rights" is a win-win game; the more civil rights are won by others, the stronger the army defending my rights becomes. My rights are not diluted when my neighbor enjoys protection from the law—he or she becomes my ally in defending the rights we all share.

## Akin to the Civil Rights Movement

For some, comparisons between the African-American civil rights movement and the movement for gay and lesbian rights seem to diminish the long black historical struggle, with all its suffering, sacrifices and endless toil. However, people of color ought to be flattered that our movement has provided so much inspiration for others, that it has been so widely imitated, and that our tactics, methods, heroines and heroes, even our songs, have been appropriated by and served as models for others.

No parallel between movements for rights is exact. African-Americans are the only Americans who were enslaved for two centuries, and people of color carry the badge of who we are on their faces. But we are far from the only people suffering discrimination—sadly, so do many others. They deserve the law's protections and civil rights, too.

Sexual disposition parallels race—I was born black and had no choice. I couldn't change and wouldn't change if I could. Like race, our sexuality isn't a preference—it is immutable, unchangeable, and the Constitution protects us all against prejudices and discrimination based on immutable differences.

Many gays and lesbians worked side by side with me in the '60s civil rights movement. Am I to now tell them "thanks" for risking life and limb helping me win my rights—but they are excluded because of a condition of their birth? That they cannot share now in the victories they helped to win? That having accepted and embraced them as partners in a common struggle, I can now turn my back on them and deny them rights they helped me win, that I enjoy because of them?

Not a chance.

In 1965, those of us who worked in the civil rights movement were buoyed by a radio address given by Lyndon Johnson. His words speak to us today. He said then,

> It is difficult to fight for freedom. But I also know how difficult it can be to bend long years of habit and custom to grant it. There is no room for injustice anywhere in the American mansion. But there is always room for understanding those who see the old ways crumbling. And to them today I simply say this: It must come. It is right that it should come. And when it has, you will find a burden has been lifted from your shoulders too. It is not just a question of guilt, although there is that. It is that men cannot live with a lie and not be stained by it.

One lesson of the civil rights movement of yesterday—and the ongoing civil rights movement of today—is that the simplest of ordinary acts—taking a seat on a bus or a lunch counter, registering to vote, applying for a marriage license—can have extraordinary ramifications. It can change our world, change the way we act and think.

Thank you again for this honor.

The old ways are crumbling.

Let us leave here determined to fight on until they do.

It must come.

> *"Defining marriage as the union of a man and a woman would not deny homosexuals the basic civil rights accorded to other citizens."*

# Opposing Same-Sex Marriage Does Not Discriminate Against Gays

*Timothy J. Dailey*

*In the following viewpoint, Timothy J. Dailey contends that defining marriage as the union of a man and a woman does not discriminate against homosexuals because marriage is not a right. Dailey contends that gay marriages are not the equivalent of traditional marriages and that homosexuality is unnatural. Banning gay marriage, says Dailey, is necessary to protect the institutions of marriage and family. Dailey is a senior fellow for the conservative Christian organization, the Family Research Council.*

As you read, consider the following questions:

1. What sci-fi novel inspired the polyamory movement?

2. What three reasons does Dailey use to support his contention that same-sex relationships are not the equivalent of marriage?

3. What did the Minnesota Supreme Court find in the case *Baker v. Nelson?*

In what some call a denial of a basic civil right, a Missouri man has been told he may not marry his long-term companion. Although his situation is unique, the logic of his argument is remarkably similar to that employed by advocates of homosexual marriage.

The man claims that the essential elements of marriage—love and commitment—are indeed present: "She's gorgeous. She's sweet. She's loving. I'm very proud of her. . . . Deep down, way down, I'd love to have children with her."

Why is the state of Missouri, as well as the federal government, displaying such heartlessness in denying the holy bonds of wedlock to this man and his would-be "wife"?

It seems the state of Missouri is not prepared to indulge a man who waxes eloquent about his love for a 22-year-old mare named Pixel.

## The Threat to Marriage

The Missouri man and homosexual "marriage" proponents categorically reject the definition of marriage as the union of a man and a woman. Instead, the sole criterion for marriage becomes the presence of "love" and "mutual commitment." But once marriage is no longer confined to a man and a woman, it is impossible to exclude virtually any relationship between two or more partners of either sex—even non-human "partners."

To those who object to comparing gay marriage to widely-rejected sexual preferences, it should be pointed out that until very recent times the very suggestion that two men or two women could "marry" was itself greeted with scorn.

Of course, media stories on same-sex marriage rarely address the fact that redefining marriage logically leads to the Missouri man and his mare. Instead, media reports typically focus instead on homosexual couples who resemble the stereotypical ideal of a married couple. Ignored in such reports is social science research indicating that such idealized "families" are utterly atypical among homosexuals. . . .

## The "Polyamory" Movement

The movement to redefine marriage has found full expression in what is variously called "polyfidelity" or "polyamory," which seeks to replace traditional marriage with a bewildering array of sexual combinations between various groups of individuals.

"Polyamory" is derived from Greek and Latin roots, and is loosely translated "many loves." Polyamorists reject the "myth" of monogamy and claim to practice "harmonious love and intimacy between multiple poly partners." Stanley Kurtz describes the "bewildering variety of sexual combinations. There are triads of one woman and two men; heterosexual group marriages; groups in which some or all members are bisexual; lesbian groups, and so forth."

The polyamory movement took its inspiration from Robert Heinlein's 1961 sci-fi novel, *Stranger in a Strange Land*, in which sexual possessiveness (as in marital exclusivity) is portrayed as an evil leading to societal ills such as murder and war. The book helped spawn a number of ill-fated sexual communes, such as San Francisco's Kerista community, in which members had sexual relations with each other according to a rotating schedule.

The Kerista commune collapsed in 1992, but the polyamory movement has taken hold in academia where, according to *First Things*, its proponents "are now so influential, if not dominant, in the academic field of marriage and family law." Scholars enamored with polyamory argue in favor of "a social revolution that would replace traditional marriage and family law."

Kurtz concurs that the "gradual transition from gay marriage to state-sanctioned polyamory, and the eventual abolition of marriage itself, is now the most influential paradigm within academic family law." One prominent advocate of polyamory, David Chambers, professor of law at the University of Michigan, argues: "By ceasing to conceive of marriage as a partnership composed of one person of each sex, the state may become more receptive to units of three or more."

## The Frat House Concept of "Family"

This radical definition of marriage gives rise to bizarre conceptions of family that include virtually any relationship or social group. In 1990, a San Francisco task force on family policy led by lesbian activist Roberta Achtenberg defined the family as a "unit of interdependent and interacting persons, related together over time by strong social and emotional bonds and/or by ties of marriage, birth, and adoption."

Polyamory advocates pay scant attention to the dangers posed to children being raised according to this "frat house with revolving bedroom doors" concept of marriage and the family. Yet, this nebulous, free-for-all model of the family looms ahead for our society unless a bulwark is created in the form of a constitutional amendment protecting marriage.

The slippery slope leading to the destruction of marriage as we know it draws ever closer with the decision of the Massachusetts Supreme Judicial Court to compel the state legislature to grant homosexual sex partners the legal status of married people. This decision has emboldened public officials in various localities to grant marriage licenses to homosexual couples, igniting a national debate on the question: What is marriage—and where do we draw the limits on who can marry?

# Same-Sex Relationships Are Not the Equivalent of Marriage

A growing body of research indicates that in key respects homosexual and lesbian relationships are radically different than married couples.

- Relationship duration: While a high percentage of married couples remain married for up to 20 years or longer, with many remaining wedded for life, the vast majority of homosexual relationships are short-lived and transitory. This has nothing to do with alleged "societal oppression." A study in the Netherlands, a gay-tolerant nation that has legalized homosexual marriage, found the average duration of a homosexual relationship to be one and a half years.

- Monogamy versus promiscuity: Studies indicate that while three-quarters or more of married couples remain faithful to each other, homosexual couples typically engage in a shocking degree of promiscuity. The same Dutch study found that "committed" homosexual couples have an average of eight sexual partners (outside of the relationship) per year.

- Intimate partner violence: homosexual and lesbian couples experience by far the highest levels of intimate partner violence compared with married couples as well as cohabiting heterosexual couples. Lesbians, for example, suffer a much higher level of violence than do married women.

## What About the Children?

In his exhaustive examination of human history, Giovanni Battista Vico (1668–1744), Professor of Rhetoric at the University of Naples, concluded that marriage between a man and a woman is an essential characteristic of civilization, and as such is the "seedbed" of society. Vico warned that chaos would ensue in the absence of strong social norms encouraging marital faithfulness and the loving care of children born to the union.

Since reproduction requires a male and a female, society will always depend upon heterosexual marriage to provide the "seedbed" of future generations. The evidence indicates that homosexual or lesbian households are not a suitable environment for children.

Data from the 2000 U.S. Census and other sources indicates that only a small percentage of homosexual households choose to raise children. One reason for this is that the raising of children is inimical to the typical homosexual lifestyle, which as we have seen typically involves a revolving bedroom door. With the added problem of high rates of intimate partner violence, such households constitute a dangerous and unstable environment for children.

## Gay Households with Children

Homosexuals and lesbians are unsuitable role models for children because of their lifestyle. Dr. Brad Hayton observes that homosexual households "model a poor view of marriage to children. They are taught by example and belief that marital relationships are transitory and mostly sexual in nature. . . . And they are taught that monogamy in a marriage is not the norm [and] should be discouraged if one wants a good 'marital' relationship."

## The Phony Comparison with Race

Many black Americans are understandably offended when gay activists, who have never been relegated to the back of a bus, equate their agenda with racial discrimination. In a statement supporting traditional marriage, several black pastors wrote: "We find the gay community's attempt to tie their pursuit of special rights based on their behavior to the civil rights movement of the 1960s and 1970s abhorrent."

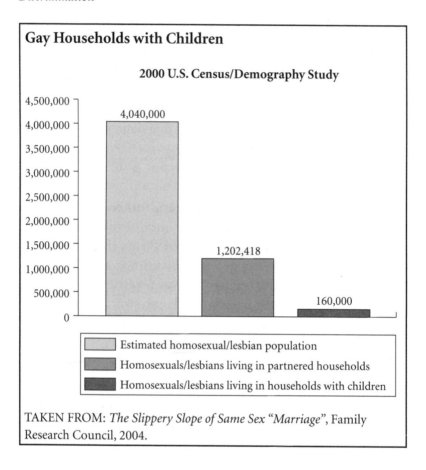

Gay Households with Children

2000 U.S. Census/Demography Study

- Estimated homosexual/lesbian population
- Homosexuals/lesbians living in partnered households
- Homosexuals/lesbians living in households with children

TAKEN FROM: *The Slippery Slope of Same Sex "Marriage"*, Family Research Council, 2004.

A majority of Black Americans reject the facile comparison of sexual behavior with an immutable characteristic such as race, and disagree with the oft-heard contention by gay activists that homosexuals are "born that way." A Pew Research poll found that by an overwhelming 61 to 26 percent margin, Black Protestants believe sexual orientation can be changed. The same poll reported that Black Americans oppose homosexual marriage by a 60 to 28 percent margin.

## Gay Marriage Is Not a Civil Rights Issue

Defining marriage as the union of a man and a woman would not deny homosexuals the basic civil rights accorded other citizens. Nowhere in the Bill of Rights or in any legislation proceeding from it are homosexuals excluded from the rights enjoyed by all citizens—including the right to marry.

However, no citizen has the unrestricted right to marry whoever they want. A parent cannot marry their child (even if he or she is of age), two or more spouses, or the husband or wife of another person. Such restrictions are based upon the accumulated wisdom not only of Western civilization but also of societies and cultures around the world for millennia.

Neither can gay activists appeal to a "natural rights" argument: i.e., no reasonable person would deny homosexuals and lesbians their self-evident right to marry. Harry Jaffa cogently replies that such arguments actually argue *against* homosexual marriage: "Nature and reason tell us that a Negro is a human being, and is not to be treated like a horse or an ox or a dog, just as they tell us that a Jew is a human being, and is not to be treated as a plague-bearing bacillus. But with the very same voice, nature and reason tell us that a man is not a woman, and that sexual friendship is properly between members of opposite-sexes, not the same sex."

## Upholding Traditional Marriage Is Not "Discrimination"

Discrimination occurs when someone is unjustly denied some benefit or opportunity. But it must first be demonstrated that such persons deserve to be treated equally. For example, FAA [Federal Aviation Administration] and airline regulations rightly discriminate regarding who is allowed into the cockpit of an airline. Those who are not trained pilots have no rightful claim to "discrimination" because they are not allowed to fly an airplane.

On the other hand, discrimination would occur if properly credentialed pilots are refused hiring simply because of the color of their skin. In this case such individuals have been denied employment simply because of their race.

The issue of alleged discrimination was addressed by the Minnesota Supreme Court in *Baker v. Nelson*, when it rejected the argument that denying a same-sex couple the right to marry was the equivalent of racial discrimination. The court found: "In common sense and constitutional sense, there is a clear distinction between a marital restriction based merely upon race and one based upon the fundamental difference in sex."

Similarly, in October 2003, a three-judge panel of the Arizona Court of Appeals ruled unanimously against two homosexuals who argued in a lawsuit that marriage is a fundamental right, and that prohibiting it for same-sex couples violates constitutional protections for due process. The court found that the state's ban on homosexual marriage "rationally furthers a legitimate state interest," and thus does not discriminate against homosexuals by depriving them of their constitutional rights. The court further noted: "Recognizing a right to marry someone of the same sex would not expand the established right to marry, but would redefine the legal meaning of 'marriage.'"

When gay activists and their supporters cry "discrimination!" they conveniently avoid the question of whether homosexual relationships merit being granted equality with marriage. Yet this question deserves our close examination, for the danger posed to our society by redefining marriage is no less than permitting unqualified individuals to fly airplanes.

# Periodical Bibliography

The following articles have been selected to supplement the diverse views presented in this chapter.

Mark Buchanan      "Are We Born Prejudiced? We Know Ethnic Prejudice Is Wrong, So How Come it's Still Rife," *New Scientist*, March 17, 2007.

David J. Connor and Beth A. Ferri      "Integration and Inclusion—A Troubling Nexus: Race, Disability, and Special Education," *Journal of African American History*, Winter– Spring 2005.

Cornelia Dean      "Bias Is Hurting Women In Science, Panel Reports," *New York Times*, September 19, 2006.

Edward Guthmann      "Shelby Steele Has a Lot to Say About Black Society. He Calls It Common Sense. Some Call Him an Uncle Tom," *San Francisco Chronicle*, May 15, 2006.

Greg Mathis      "Black Men Must Fight Back Against Obstacles," *Ebony*, February 2007.

Betsy Morris      "How Corporate America is Betraying Women," *Fortune*, January 10, 2005.

Michael Olneck      "Economic Consequences of the Academic Achievement Gap for African Americans," *Marquette Law Review*, Fall 2005.

Jonathan Rauch      "Social Studies: A Pariah's Triumph—and America's," *National Journal*, December 1, 2006.

Deborah L. Rhode      "Gender-Based Bias Engenders Action," *New Jersey Law Journal*, June 13, 2005.

Paul Varnell      "Why 'Just' Discrimination Isn't," *Chicago Free Press*, January 3, 2007.

# CHAPTER 2

# How Does Discrimination Impact American Society?

# Chapter Preface

The Web site www.immigrationcounters.com has a counter that registers the number of illegal aliens in the United States. It goes up by one every minute or so. According to the Web site on July 26, 2007, there were 21,081,246 illegal immigrants in the United States and counting. A more conventional and reliable source, the Pew Hispanic Center, puts the number of illegal aliens at about 12 million. Immigration, particularly illegal immigration, is a contentious and emotional issue in the United States. On the one side are those who feel that illegal immigrants are draining public funds, taking jobs away from Americans, contributing to crime, and threatening traditional American values. On the other side are those that feel that all Americans—except Native Americans—are immigrants and that immigrants strengthen American society and contribute to the rich culture of the United States. One of the most contentious issues about immigration is how it affects the wages and employment opportunities of U.S. workers. Some people want to force employers to verify the immigration status of their workers to prevent illegal immigrants from living and working in the United States; however, other people believe that requiring worker verification will lead to discrimination against immigrants.

Many Americans believe that illegal immigrants displace thousands of American workers every year and reduce the wages of other American workers. *Washington Times* columnists John Hostettler and Lamar Smith contend that "when there are many willing workers, employers cut wages. That is simple supply and demand. Illegal immigrants who take low-skilled jobs reduce wages and take jobs from both citizens and legal immigrants." Those who oppose this position point to a study that looked at the impact of immigrants (both legal and illegal) on the workforce in California—the state with the highest share of immigrants. The study by economist Giovanni Peri, published by the California Public Policy Insitute, could find no evidence that the influx of immigrants over the period 1960–2004 worsened the employment opportunities of Americans. Additionally, Peri found that during 1990–2004, immigration actually increased the wages of Americans in California by 4 percent.

Many people believe that illegal immigrants are able to work in the United States illegally because they obtain counterfeit documents and employers do not verify the authenticity of their documents. Says Heather Mac Donald, an editor with New York's *City Journal*, the "hiring practices in illegal-immigrant-saturated industries are a charade. Millions of illegal workers pretend to present valid documents, and thousands of employers pretend to believe them. The law doesn't require the employer to verify that a worker is actually qualified to work, and as long as the proffered documents are not patently phony—scrawled with red crayon on a matchbook, say—the employer will nearly always be exempt from liability merely by having eyeballed them." Former Massachusetts governor Mitt Romney said the federal government needs to "develop a system where residency and citizenship documents are tamper-proof, and employers can tap into a nationwide verification network to check on employees' immigration status." Those that favor worker verification systems say they will help stem the flow of illegal immigrants into the country.

Others believe the process of worker verification is ripe for discrimination. Worker verification systems are typically dependent on the Social Security database, which is estimated to contain millions of errors. Additionally, in pilot systems studying worker verification systems, employers were often found to use the system improperly and sometimes discriminatorily. Testifying in front of the U.S. Senate Judiciary Committee in June 2006, Cecilia Muñoz of the National Council of La Raza said, "It is well documented that one result of employer sanctions and worker verification has been increased discrimination against persons who look or sound 'foreign' or have a 'foreign' surname. Some employers demand that certain workers show additional or 'better' documents beyond what is required in the law; often asking for immigration documents from U.S. citizens whom they perceive to be immigrants. Other employers implement unlawful 'citizen only' policies." Those who oppose worker verification systems say that the potential for wide spread employer discrimination against immigrant workers is too great a price to pay to reduce illegal immigration.

As of summer 2007, U.S. lawmakers have not established a nationwide worker verification system. The immigration debate illustrates how discrimination can impact American society. The authors of the viewpoints in the following chapter explore other issues involving discrimination and its impact on in the United States.

*"Profiling of Arabs and Muslims amounts to selective enforcement of the law against anyone with a certain type of 'swarthy' foreign-looking appearance even if they do not in fact fit the terrorist profile."*

# Racial Profiling Against Muslims to Prevent Terrorism Is Ineffective and Discriminatory

**Leadership Conference on Civil Rights Education Fund**

*In this viewpoint, the Leadership Conference on Civil Rights Education Fund (LCCREF) argues the ineffectiveness of racial profiling. The authors contend that focusing on particular ethnic groups, rather than behavioral patterns, misdirects attention from the real offenders, who may or may not be of the expected ethnic background. Meanwhile, those who are targeted may be peaceful, law-abiding members of society. The LCCREF further asserts that people wary of profiling will lay low to avoid unwanted trouble and may never come forward with information the United States needs to combat terrorism effectively. The*

Leadership Conference on Civil Rights Education Fund, "Wrong Then, Wrong Now: Racial Profiling Before & After September 11, 2001," *civilrights.org*, February 27, 2003. Reproduced by permission.

*LCCREF, the education and research arm of the Leadership Conference on Civil Rights, strives to educate the public of injustices and to promote national policies that support civil rights.*

As you read, consider the following questions:

1. What is one of the examples of terrorist activity the authors cite when the profiling of Arabs would not have been effective?

2. On what might investigators focus if not on physical characteristics, according to the LCCREF?

3. What does Khaled Saffuri do to avoid the hassles of racial profiling with air transportation?

The assumptions driving terrorism profiling are the same as those behind traditional, street-level profiling—i.e., that a particular crime (here, terrorism) is most likely to be committed by members of a particular racial, ethnic or religious group, and that members of that group are, in general, likely to be involved in that kind of criminal activity. . . . These assumptions are flawed.

First, it is not true that terrorist acts are necessarily perpetrated by Arabs, or that the perpetrator of a terrorist act is likely to be an Arab. While all the men involved in the September 11 hijackings were Arab nationals, Richard Reid, who on December 22, 2001, tried to ignite an explosive device on a trans-Atlantic flight, was a British citizen of Jamaican ancestry. Prior to September 11, the bloodiest act of terrorism on United States soil was perpetrated by [Oklahoma City bomber] Timothy McVeigh. Non-Arabs like John Walker Lindh can be found in the ranks of the Taliban, al Qaeda and other terrorist organizations. At the same time, the overwhelming majority of Arabs, Arab Americans, Muslims, South Asians and Sikhs are law-abiding persons who would never think of engaging in terrorism.

## Profiling Hinders the Anti-Terrorism Effort

Focusing on the many Arabs, South Asians, Muslims, and Sikhs who clearly pose no threat to national security detracts from the anti-terrorism effort. First, it diverts precious law enforcement resources away from investigations of individuals—including Arabs and Muslims—who have been linked to terrorist activity by specific and credible evidence. Second, it ignores the possibility that someone who does not fit the profile may be engaged in terrorism, or may be an unwitting accomplice to terrorism.

That race is an ineffective measure of an individual's terrorist intentions was made clear in a memorandum circulated to American law enforcement agents worldwide by a group of senior U.S. law enforcement officials in October 2002. The memorandum, entitled "Assessing Behaviors," emphasized that focusing on the racial characteristics of individuals was a waste of law enforcement resources and might cause law enforcement officials to ignore suspicious behavior, past or present, by someone who did not fit a racial profile. One of the authors of the report noted: "Fundamentally, believing that you can achieve safety by looking at characteristics instead of behaviors is silly. If your goal is preventing attacks . . . you want your eyes and ears looking for pre-attack behaviors, not characteristics."

The memorandum urged investigators to focus on actual behavior involving selection of targets, recruitment and organization of members, acquisition of skills, assessing vulnerabilities of targets, acquiring financing, probing boundaries, communicating with conspirators, using insiders, maintaining secrecy, and acquiring weapons. An emphasis on race, the memorandum noted, distracts from the observance of potentially suspicious behavior. This memorandum answers one of the main arguments of those who support racial profiling in the context of airport searches—i.e., that it is simply logical to focus precious law enforcement resources on Arab men rather than on older women from Minnesota or Swedish au pairs. What U.S. intelligence experts have made clear is that *any* emphasis on personal characteristics, rather than on behavior, misdirects scarce anti-terrorism resources.

This is not to say that law enforcement can never rely on race in fighting terrorism. As in street-level law enforcement, it is permissible to rely on race as part of a suspect-specific description. No one argues, for example, that the police cannot follow up on a specific tip that a group of Arabs is plotting terrorist acts in a particular apartment building by questioning Arabs who live in that building. Assuming the reliability of the source or the specificity of the information, identification of an individual's race carries with it the real potential for uncovering criminal activity.

Profiling, by contrast, is a scattershot device that is so crude as to be virtually useless. It is no coincidence that the questioning of 8,000 young Arab men in late 2001–early 2002 yielded virtually no leads about terrorism—there was no evidence to suggest that any of these men knew anything about terrorism in the first place.

## Applying Racial Profiles Is Difficult

Racial profiling is particularly foolish in the anti-terrorism context for three additional reasons. First, even if one accepts the false assumption that terrorists are likely to be Arab or Muslim, the *application* of the profile is fraught with error. . . . Many persons who are neither Arab nor Muslim can get caught up in the terrorism profiling web. Consider these other examples from the airport security context:

- On October 22, 2001, four Hispanic businessmen were escorted off a Delta flight after passengers alerted airline staff that the men appeared to be Middle Eastern.

- On September 26, 2001, a group of six passengers of Indian ethnicity were questioned aboard a United Airlines flight from Los Angeles to Washington, D.C. The men were taken to the back of the plane, where they were first questioned by a pilot and then by FBI and INS [Immigration and Naturalization Service].

• On September 24, 2001, a Canadian woman of Indian origin was removed from her US Airways flight from Toronto to Las Vegas because her last name was similar in pronunciation to the name of one of the September 11 hijackers, Mohammed Atta. She was told that her name was "Middle Eastern" and therefore suspicious.

• A flight bound for New York's LaGuardia Airport was accompanied on its descent by a military plane after a passenger raised suspicions about a group of entertainers from India who were passing notes and changing seats. The group was detained for questioning and released five hours later without being charged. The passengers were not terrorists; they were animated because they were excited about visiting New York.

Thus, the profile of a terrorist as an Arab or Muslim has been applied to individuals who are neither Arab nor Muslim (e.g., Hispanics, Indians, and Sikhs). Profiling of Arabs and Muslims amounts to selective enforcement of the law against anyone with a certain type of "swarthy" foreign-looking appearance even if they do not in fact fit the terrorist profile. The profile is then useless in fighting terrorism, as well as offensive to an ever-broadening category of persons.

## Terrorist Organizations Are Adaptable

Second, using racial profiling in the anti-terrorism effort is a classic example of refighting the last war. As noted above, al Qaeda and other terrorist organizations are pan-ethnic: they include Asians, Anglos, and ethnic Europeans. They are also adaptive, dynamic organizations that will learn how to use

## Flying While Muslim

... [A]ttractive and logical as it may seem to a fearful traveling public, a profiling policy focusing on people who appear to be "flying while Muslim" would be extraordinarily difficult to implement and counterproductive.

There are more than 1 billion Muslims in the world—a huge population to single out for special scrutiny—and only a tiny fraction are members of Al Qaeda or other terrorist groups. And focusing on Muslims would ignore the fact that terrorists professing adherence to other religions have claimed many lives over the years as well, and will certainly do so again in the future.

Even if the goal of security were mistakenly limited to identifying Muslims, the task would be complicated by the fact that Muslims come from nearly all countries in the world, and from every racial group. Many have identifiably Muslim names, but others do not—and names can be changed, legally or with fake identification documents.

*K. Jack Riley and Greg Ridgeway,*
*"Racial Profiling Won't Stop Terror,"*
washingtonpost.com, *October 11, 2006.*

non-Arabs such as Richard Reid to carry out terrorist attacks, or to smuggle explosive devices onto planes in the luggage of innocent people. The fact that the September 11 hijackers were Arab means little in predicting who the next terrorists will be. Racial profiling in any case is a crude mechanism; against an enemy like al Qaeda it is virtually useless.

## Profiling Alienates Possible Information Sources

Third, and perhaps most important, the use of profiling in the anti-terrorism context, as in the street-crime context, alienates the very people that federal authorities have deemed instrumental in the anti-terrorism fight. Arab, South Asian, and Muslim communities may yield useful information to those fighting terrorism. Arabs and Arab Americans also offer the government an important source of Arabic speakers and translators. The singling out of Arabs, South Asians, Muslims, and Sikhs for investigation regardless of whether any credible evidence links them to terrorism will simply alienate these individuals and compromise the anti-terrorism effort. In particular, to the extent that federal authorities use the anti-terrorism effort as a pretext for detaining or deporting immigration law violators, individuals who might have information that is useful against terrorism may be afraid to come forward. At a minimum, those individuals will choose not to register, thereby defeating the very purpose of the registration program.

The alienation that results from terrorism profiling is compounded by the clumsy and insensitive manner in which it has thus far been carried out. . . . Arabs, South Asians, Muslims, and Sikhs who have tried to cooperate with authorities and to comply with the law have consistently been met by verbal (and sometimes physical) abuse; complete insensitivity to their cultural and religious practices; and a general lack of respect. . . . This treatment has caused many Arabs, South Asians, Muslims, and Sikhs to alter their behavior in order to avoid confrontations with authorities. Khaled Saffuri, a Lebanese man living in Great Falls, Virginia, says he makes sure to shave closely and wear a suit every time he flies; stays silent during flights and makes sure not to go to the bathroom in the middle of the flight; and sometimes avoids flying altogether in favor of long drives to his destinations in order to avoid air travel. In October 2002, Canada even issued a travel advisory warning those of its citizens born in Middle Eastern countries against traveling to the United States because of the hassles they would encounter. One celebrated Canadian, author Rohinton Mistry, who is of Indian descent and neither Arab nor

Muslim, cancelled his book tour of the United States because he was "repeatedly and rudely" stopped at each airport along his tour route.

## A Track Record of Failure

Recent events have demonstrated the futility of relying on profiles to predict who engages in targeted violence. In the fall of 2002, the Washington, D.C., area was shaken by a series of sniper attacks. Traditional profiles of serial killers assume that they are disaffected White men. Of course, the two men charged with the attacks are Black—an African American Gulf War Veteran, John Allen Muhammad, and Jamaican-born John Lee Malvo. Their capture was hailed by law enforcement authorities as a triumph of "old fashioned police work" and entailed the investigation of multiple leads, the pursuit of evidence nationwide, and the use of the media and the public to help develop the facts. The investigation showed how reliance on a profile "can have [police] chasing a stereotype while the real culprit slips away."

Profiling has proven to be an inaccurate indicator of other types of targeted violent crimes. Traditional profiles presumed that political assassins were male. But women—Sarah Jane Moore and Lynette "Squeaky" Fromm—carried out assassination attempts on the life of President [Gerald] Ford. And in a situation directly analogous to the one facing Arabs and Muslims today, the 10 individuals found to be spying for Japan during World War II were Caucasian. They clearly did not fit the profile that caused America to order the internment of thousands of Japanese Americans.

## Old-Fashioned Methods Are Still Best

The same kind of old-fashioned police work that tracks down serial killers, assassins, and spies will help catch terrorists, not reliance on broad, inaccurate, and confusing racial stereotypes. Federal authorities have also taken many useful steps to improve airport security that pose no threat to civil rights. The use of improved technology to detect explosives, luggage matching protocols, better training of screeners, and reinforcing of cockpit doors, for example, are all prudent measures to enhance airport security. *These* are the types of weapons, along with behavior-based surveillance, that will win the war against terrorism.

Those who support the use of profiling against Arabs, South Asians, Muslims, and Sikhs argue that America must resort to profiling given the stakes. The opposite is in fact true. The stakes are so high that the nation cannot afford to use an anti-terrorism mechanism as deeply flawed as racial profiling.

*"It is unfortunate that loyal Muslims or Arabs might be burdened because of terrorists who share their race, nationality or religion. But any inconvenience is preferable to suffering a second mass terrorist attack on American soil."*

# Racial Profiling of Muslims Is Justified to Prevent Terrorism

*Michelle Malkin*

*National security justifies profiling based on race, religion, or nationality, asserts Michelle Malkin in the following viewpoint. Malkin points to missed opportunities to use racial profiling before 9/11 that might have prevented the attacks on the World Trade Center in New York. She claims Middle Eastern terrorists led by Osama Bin Laden will attempt more attacks on the United States and racial profiling is an effective tool to thwart them. Malkin, a syndicated columnist and political commentator, has written several books on terrorism.*

As you read, consider the following questions:

1. According to Malkin, ethnic activists and civil-liberties groups support racial profiling in what instance?

Michelle Malkin, "Racial Profiling: A Matter of Survival," *USA Today*, August 16, 2004. www.usatoday.com. Reproduced by permission of Michelle Malkin and Creators Syndicate, Inc.

2. What was one of the reasons FBI director Robert Mueller gave for not investigating militant Muslim men before 9/11?

3. According to Malkin, instead of focusing exclusively on the 12 Muslim chaplains, the Pentagon did what?

When our national security is on the line, "racial profiling"—or more precisely, threat profiling based on race, religion or nationality—is justified. Targeted intelligence-gathering at mosques and in local Muslim communities, for example, makes perfect sense when we are at war with Islamic extremists.

Yet, last week, the FBI came under fire for questioning Muslims in Seattle about possible terrorist ties. Members of a local mosque complained to [U.S.] Rep. Jim McDermott, who called for a congressional investigation of the FBI's innocuous tactics. The American Civil Liberties Union of Washington accused the agency of "ethnic profiling."

But where else are federal agents supposed to turn for help in uncovering terrorist plots by Islamic fanatics: Buddhist temples? Knights of Columbus meetings? Amish neighborhoods?

Some might argue that profiling is so offensive to fundamental American values that it ought to be prohibited, even if the prohibition jeopardizes our safety. Yet many of the ethnic activists and civil-liberties groups who object most strenuously to the use of racial, ethnic, religious and nationality classifications during war support the use of similar classifications to ensure "diversity" or "parity" in peacetime.

The civil-rights hypocrites have never met a "compelling government interest" for using racial, ethnicity or nationality classifications they didn't like, except when that compelling interest happens to be the nation's very survival.

## Flying Imams Lawsuit

The "flying imams'" federal lawsuit, filed [in March 2007] in Minneapolis, has made headlines around the country. The imams are demanding unspecified damages from US Airways and the Metropolitan Airports Commission, both with deep pockets. . . .

Recall the November 2006 incident that gave rise to the suit. The imams engaged in a variety of suspicious behaviors while boarding a US Airways flight, according to the airport police report. Some prayed loudly in the gate area, spoke angrily about the United States and Saddam, switched seats and sat in the 9/11 hijackers' configuration, and unnecessarily requested seatbelt extenders that could be used as weapons, according to witness reports and US Airways spokeswoman Andrea Rader.

After extensive consultations, the pilot asked authorities to remove the imams for questioning, which they did, releasing them later that day. . . .

Their lawsuit appears to be the latest component in a national campaign to intimidate airlines and government agencies from acting prudently to ensure passenger safety. The Council on American-Islamic Relations, which is advising the imams, is also calling for congressional hearings and promoting federal legislation to "end racial profiling" in air travel. If the legislation passes, airport personnel who disproportionately question passengers who are Muslim or of Middle Eastern origin could be subject to sanctions.

*Katherine Kersten, "Think Again with Katherine Kersten:*
*The Real Target of the 6 Imams' Discrimination Suit,"*
Minneapolis Star Tribune, *March 14, 2007. www.startribune.com.*

## Profiling Might Have Prevented 9/11

Consider what happened in summer 2001, when Phoenix FBI agent Kenneth Williams urged his superiors to investigate militant Muslim men whom he suspected of training in U.S. flight schools as part of al-Qaeda missions.

Williams' recommendation was rejected, FBI Director Robert Mueller later said, partly because of concerns that the plan could be viewed as discriminatory racial profiling.

Mueller acknowledged that if Williams' Phoenix profiling memo had been shared with the agency's Minneapolis office, which had unsuccessfully sought a special intelligence warrant to search suspected terrorist Zacarias Moussaoui's laptop computer, the warrant might have been granted.

If the FBI had taken Williams' advice, the feeling of some Arabs and Muslims might have been hurt. But the Twin Towers might still be standing and 3,000 innocent people might be alive today.

Absolutists who oppose national-security profiling often invoke the World War II experience of Japanese-Americans. When asked whether the 12 Muslim chaplains serving in the armed forces should be vetted more carefully than military rabbis or priests, Sarah Eltantawi of the Muslim Public Affairs Council raised the specter of Japanese internment.

The analogy is ridiculous. The more extensive screening of 12 military officers is a far cry from the evacuation of 112,000 individuals on the West Coast. The targeted profiling of Muslims serving in sensitive positions is not a constitutional crisis.

Some argue that the dismissal of charges against Army Capt. James Yee, a former Muslim chaplain who ministered to enemy combatants at Guantanamo Bay, Cuba, and was initially suspected of espionage, undermines the case for profiling of any kind. Not at all. As the Defense Department has acknowledged, the military's 12 Muslim chaplains were trained by a radical Wahhabi school and were certified by a Muslim group founded by Abdurahman Alamoudi, who was charged in September 2003 with accepting hundreds of thousands of dollars from Libya, a U.S.-designated sponsor of terrorism. These associations cannot be ignored.

Unfortunately, the Pentagon caved in to Eltantawi and her fellow travelers. Rather than focus exclusively on the 12 Muslim chaplains, it pressed forward with a review of all 2,800 military chaplains.

The refusal to be discriminating was, as [U.S.] Sen. Jon Kyl, acknowledged, the "height of politically correct stupidity."

In the wake of 9/11, opponents of profiling have shifted away from arguing against it because it is "racist" and now claim that it endangers security because it is a drain on resources and damages relations with ethnic and religious minorities, thereby hampering intelligence-gathering. These assertions are cleverly fine-tuned to appeal to post-9/11 sensibilities, but they are unfounded and disingenuous. The fact that al-Qaeda is using some non-Arab recruits does not render profiling moot. As long as we have open borders, Osama bin Laden will continue to send Middle East terrorists here by land, sea and air. Profiling is just one discretionary investigative tool among many.

Post-9/11, the belief that racial, religious and nationality profiling is never justified has become a dangerous bugaboo. It is unfortunate that loyal Muslims or Arabs might be burdened because of terrorists who share their race, nationality or religion. But any inconvenience is preferable to suffering a second mass terrorist attack on American soil.

| "[R]ecent medical research (also) shows that racial and ethnic minority patients tend to receive a lower quality of care than non-minorities, even when they have the same types of health insurance."

# Discrimination Leads to Healthcare Disparities

*Institute of Medicine*

*In this viewpoint, written by the researchers at the Institute of Medicine (IOM), the authors claim that racial and ethnic minorities receive poorer healthcare than white people. Asked by the U.S. Congress to investigate racial and ethnic disparities in healthcare, the IOM found that several factors contribute to the disparities. Among them are cost containment policies at hospitals, patients' own attitudes and behaviors, and healthcare providers' biases, prejudices, and uncertainty when treating minorities. The IOM said that the quality of healthcare for minorities can be enhanced when minority patients ask questions and become educated about what to expect during healthcare exams. The IOM is part of the National Academy of Sciences and advises the president and the U.S. Congress on medical issues.*

Institute of Medicine, "What Healthcare Consumers Need to Know About Racial and Ethnic Disparities in Healthcare," Institute of Medicine (IOM) Report Brief, March, 2002, pp. 1–6. Copyright © 2002 by the National Academy of Sciences. All rights reserved. Reproduced by permission.

As you read, consider the following questions:

1. How does this IOM report define healthcare disparities?

2. Explain how a doctor's uncertainty about a minority patient's condition and best course of treatment may contribute to healthcare disparities.

3. How does the IOM report define prejudice?

It is often difficult to face a visit to the doctor, even if it's just for a routine check-up. Many people find it stressful and even frightening to go to the doctor, especially when they are not feeling well. Worries about starting treatment for an illness or disease can get worse when people think about how much the treatment will cost and the possibility of the doctor making a mistake. And for minority patients, there can be more issues to think about—including whether their race or ethnicity will affect the kind of care they receive.

## Racial and Ethnic Gaps in Access to Healthcare

There are wide differences between racial and ethnic groups in access to healthcare and the availability of health insurance. Minorities, especially Hispanic and African-American families, are less likely than whites to have private health insurance. Or if they have insurance, minorities are more likely than whites to be enrolled in health plans that place tight limits on the types of services that patients may receive. Also, the best quality healthcare services and providers are not always found in minority communities. These are some of the major reasons why minorities receive a lower quality of care.

But recent medical research also shows that racial and ethnic minority patients tend to receive a lower quality of care than non-minorities, even when they have the same types of health insurance.

For that reason, Congress asked the Institute of Medicine (IOM) to investigate racial and ethnic disparities in healthcare delivery. The IOM was instructed to determine how wide the healthcare gap is, identify potential reasons why it occurs, and suggest ways to eliminate it. In its final report (*Unequal Treatment: Confronting Racial and Ethnic Disparities in Healthcare*), the panel of scientists and doctors assembled by the IOM concluded that minority patients are less likely than whites to receive the same quality of heathcare, even when they have similar insurance or the ability to pay for care. To make matters worse, this healthcare gap is linked with higher death rates among minorities.

## What Are Healthcare Disparities?

The IOM report defined healthcare *disparities* as differences in the quality of care received by minorities and non-minorities who have equal access to care—that is, when these groups have similar health insurance and the same access to a doctor—*and* when there are no differences between these groups in their preferences and needs for treatment. This definition acknowledges that some differences in the quality of healthcare between minorities and whites are explainable. For example, research shows that some minority patients are more likely than whites to reject their doctor's advice for treatment, although this difference in treatment preferences is generally very small.

## What Are the Causes of Healthcare Disparities?

The IOM report found that healthcare disparities do not have one simple cause. Instead, many potential sources of healthcare disparities were discovered. Three of these sources are described below.

*The way healthcare systems are organized and operate can contribute to differences.* Sometimes healthcare systems, hospitals, or clinics adopt policies or practices that are based on good intentions—such as the need to contain healthcare costs—but may pose barriers to minority patients' ability to access care. For example, some health plans offer financial incentives to physicians to keep costs low. Keeping healthcare costs down is important, but these policies may unintentionally hurt minorities, in that cost-savings may come at the expense of patients who are least educated about their treatment options and least likely to push their doctor for more services. . . .

In addition, many health plans do not offer professional interpretation or translation services to patients that don't speak English. Professional interpretation and translation services are important to help non-English speaking patients fully participate in treatment decisions and discuss concerns with their doctor privately.

*Patients' attitudes and behaviors can contribute to disparities.* There is some evidence that patients' attitudes may contribute to disparities. Some minority patients do not trust healthcare professionals, and therefore may put off seeing a doctor until their illness is too far along to effectively treat. Others do not follow their doctor's instructions exactly. In addition, some evidence suggests that minority patients are more likely to reject or refuse their doctor's recommendations for treatment. Studies show, however, that this represents only a small percentage of minority patients, and that minorities are only slightly more likely than white patients to refuse recommended treatment.

Finally, there is evidence that *healthcare providers' biases, prejudices, and uncertainty when treating minorities can contribute to healthcare disparities.* This summary focuses on how providers' attitudes and beliefs—even those that they aren't consciously aware of—may influence the quality of patient care, and what patients can do about it.

## Doctors Need Many Different Types of Information to Make a Medical Decision

To understand how doctors may contribute to healthcare disparities, it's important to understand how they make decisions about patient care. Many of the decisions that doctors must make are made with a degree of uncertainty. This uncertainty can be related to the patient's diagnosis, how the patient may respond to treatment, whether treatment might lead to potential complications, or even the patient's long-term outlook. To make matters worse, in many healthcare settings doctors may face significant time pressures, resource constraints, and on occasion, complex medical problems that are not easily understood or solved.

Uncertainty can therefore make finding the right diagnosis and treatment plan a challenge for any doctor. But when faced with patients who are from different racial or ethnic backgrounds, doctors may find that their uncertainty about the patient's condition and best course of treatment is even greater. A doctor may be uncertain about how a particular disease (or treatment) will progress in a minority group. A patient's test results may not point to an obvious solution. Sometimes, patients don't know how to describe their symptoms, or they are nervous or embarrassed about them. In addition, many doctors don't talk to their patients in plain language; they use medical terms that are difficult to understand. These kinds of problems can lead to greater uncertainty when doctors and patients don't share the same background. And in many communities, there are additional language barriers— the doctor and patient may not speak the same language, and many healthcare systems do not employ interpreters. Also, there can be cultural misunderstandings that are separate from language problems—a patient's understanding of his or her illness may be different from a doctor's perspective. Each of these factors increases the doctor's uncertainty about what

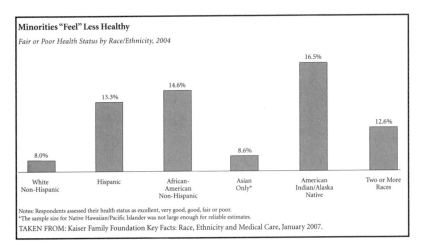

**Minorities "Feel" Less Healthy**

*Fair or Poor Health Status by Race/Ethnicity, 2004*

| White Non-Hispanic | Hispanic | African-American Non-Hispanic | Asian Only* | American Indian/Alaska Native | Two or More Races |
|---|---|---|---|---|---|
| 8.0% | 13.3% | 14.6% | 8.6% | 16.5% | 12.6% |

Notes: Respondents assessed their health status as excellent, very good, good, fair or poor.
*The sample size for Native Hawaiian/Pacific Islander was not large enough for reliable estimates.
TAKEN FROM: Kaiser Family Foundation Key Facts: Race, Ethnicity and Medical Care, January 2007.

care a patient may need. The result may be that the diagnosis and treatment plan may not be well suited to the patient's needs.

## How Are Stereotypes, Bias, and Prejudice Related to Patient Care?

Often times, the [healthcare] system gets the concept of black people off the 6 o'clock news, and they treat us all the same way. Here's a guy coming in here with no insurance. He's low breed. (African American focus group participant)

Stereotyping is a process by which people use social groups (such as sex and race) to gather, process, and recall information about other people. Stereotypes are, in other words, labels that we give to people on the basis of what groups we think they belong to.

Most people think of the word "stereotype" as a negative one, but actually these labels can be useful. Stereotyping helps people to organize a very complex world. Using them can give us more confidence in our abilities to understand a situation and respond to it. There is, however, a downside to stereotyping. It is the nature of stereotypes to be biased or unfair. They carry some level of judgment—this judgment can be positive or negative. For example, one African-American patient who had been diagnosed with diabetes reported a very negative experience. While writing a prescription, the doctor told her, "I need to write this prescription for these pills, but you'll never take them and you'll come back and tell me you're eating pig's feet and everything. . . ." Clearly, this provider looked at this person's race and assumed she had a certain type of diet and would therefore ignore his advice.

It is easy to recognize negative stereotypes, such as the kinds of attitudes that we associate with bigotry. But almost everyone stereotypes others, even though most people don't even realize they do it. And, unfortunately, we live in a society that is still affected by negative attitudes between different racial and ethnic groups. So even people who would never endorse explicitly biased stereotypes—who truly believe that they do not judge others based on social categories—have been unconsciously influenced by the *implicitly* biased stereotypes in American society.

## Stereotypes May Influence Medical Decisions

> My name is . . . [a common Hispanic surname] and when they see that name, I think there is . . . some kind of a prejudice of the name . . . We're talking about on the phone, there's a lack of respect. There's a lack of acknowledging the person and making one feel welcome. All of the courtesies that go with the profession that they are paid to do are kind of put aside. They think they can get away with a lot because "Here's another dumb Mexian." (Hispanic focus group participant)

Both implicit and explicit stereotypes shape our personal interactions. They affect how we recall information and guide our expectations and perceptions. The subtle clues we give about our own stereotypes—and how we interpret those given by others—can even produce "self-fulfilling prophecies" in social situations. That is, our own beliefs about how a situation should or will unfold can actually influence the interaction so that it meets our expectations. For example, a doctor's conscious or subconscious stereotypes about whether minority patients will stick to treatment plans or keep follow-up appointments can convey the message that the doctor doesn't expect the patient to cooperate.

## Prejudice Is Not Always Recognized or Deliberate

> If you speak English well, then an American doctor, they will treat you better. If you speak Chinese and your English is not that good, they would also kind of look down on you. They would [be] kind of prejudiced. (Chinese-American focus group participant)

Prejudice can also affect the quality of healthcare that minorities receive. Prejudice is defined as an unjustified negative attitude based on a person's group membership. Such a negative attitude is often revealed through explicitly biased stereotypes. It is a sad fact that the majority of white Americans hold prejudicial attitudes about minorities. Survey results indicate that as many as one-half to three-quarters of whites believe minorities are less intelligent, prefer to live on welfare, or are more prone to violence than white people. Yet most of these people do not recognize their attitudes as prejudice.

It's likely that most healthcare providers are not overtly prejudiced. After all, they have dedicated their lives to helping people stay well. But like many people, healthcare providers may not recognize evidence of prejudice in their own behavior.

## There Are Ways to Correct These Disparities

It may seem like an unbreakable cycle, but it is not a hopeless situation. The first step toward correcting the problem is to make people aware of it. Surveys show that, by and large, the general public is unaware that minorities receive a lower quality of care than whites. Many physicians, too, are unaware of the extent of racial and ethnic disparities in care. Greater awareness is likely to lead to more public and professional concern to solve the problem.

Awareness of the problem is not enough, however, to eliminate healthcare disparities. Wide-ranging strategies need to be aimed at state and federal health policy, policies and practices of health systems, and training of healthcare providers. These strategies should be developed and put into place at the same time. Addressing only one strategy at a time will not solve the problem.

For example, healthcare systems can take steps to help minority patients to better access care and make sure that high quality care is provided to all patients. In communities where there are a large number of people that prefer to use languages other than English, translation services can help patients feel more comfortable and that their needs are being heard. Healthcare systems can also take steps to improve relationships between doctors and patients. If each patient has a specific provider that they are able to see when they need care, the two are often able to overcome cultural barriers. This may help patients trust their provider and feel confident in following medical advice. . . .

Education is also important. First, doctors and other healthcare providers have to recognize that disparities exist, despite their best intentions. More importantly, doctors and other providers should receive *cross-cultural education*. This kind of training is designed to teach providers how cultural and social factors influence healthcare. It helps providers understand how to interact with patients who have different cultural points of view in general and, in particular, different attitudes about healthcare. It also helps providers talk to and interact with these patients in a more effective way. . . .

## Patients Can Make a Difference in Their Own Care, Starting Right Away

Patients can also make positive changes. There is some evidence to show that patient education efforts can make a difference. Books, pamphlets, and Internet sites teach patients what to expect during exams and provide information about communicating with providers. When patients are able to ask questions and get answers they understand, they are able to participate in making medical decisions. Providing patient education materials is an important step for healthcare systems; using them is an important step for patients.

> "We conclude that the studies examined
> by the IOM [Institute of Medicine]
> panel . . . fail to make a persuasive case
> that physician bias is a significant cause
> of disparate care or health status."

# Discrimination Is
# Not the Cause of
# Healthcare Disparities

## Jonathan Klick and Sally Satel

*In the following viewpoint, Jonathan Klick and Sally Satel argue that the primary cause of healthcare disparities between minorities and whites is socioeconomic status and not doctor prejudice or discrimination. The authors assert that low-income blacks receive about the same quality of healthcare as low-income whites. They contend that healthcare policy in the United States should not focus on racial disparities; since this is divisive and counterproductive. Instead, the focus should be on improving the healthcare of all Americans—regardless of ethnicity or race. Klick is an author and Professor of Law, specializing in healthcare issues, at Florida State University. Satel is a psychiatrist, author, lecturer and a fellow at the American Enterprise Institute.*

Jonathan Klick and Sally Satel, introduction, in *The Health Disparities Myth: Diagnosing the Treatment Gap*, Washington, DC: AIE Press, 2006, pp. 1–7. Copyright © 2006 American Enterprise Institute for Public Policy Research. Reprinted with permission of *The American Enterprise*, a national magazine of politics, business, and culture (TAEmag.com).

As you read, consider the following questions:

1. The authors say that academic literature about minority healthcare usually falls into one of two categories. What are the two different categories?

2. According to national data on mortality from heart disease, adults in the bottom fourth of the income distribution are how many times more likely than those in the top to die from heart disease?

3. Did black/white infant mortality ratios increase or decrease during the period from 1980 to 2000? Explain.

Two fifty-year-old men arrive at an emergency room with acute chest pain. One is white and the other black. Will they receive the same quality of treatment and have the same chance of recovery? We hope so, but many experts today insist that their race will profoundly affect how the medical-care system deals with them, and that the black patient will get much inferior care. Is this really true? And if so, why? Are differences in treatment due to deliberate discrimination or other (less invidious) factors? This monograph critically assesses recent research bearing on these questions.

## Interest in Minority Healthcare

Interest in the determinants of minority health has grown considerably since the publication of the *Report of the Secretary's Task Force on Black and Minority Health* by the U.S. Department of Health, Education, and Welfare in 1985. The academic literature falls into two categories. One line of inquiry emphasizes overt or subtle racial discrimination by physicians. Research reports in this category assert that many physicians treat their white patients better than their minority patients on the basis of race alone. We call this the "biased-doctor model" of treatment disparities.

The other line of research focuses on the influence of so-called "third factors" that are correlated with race. These factors can influence care at the level of the health system, the physician, or both. They include, for example, variations in insurance coverage (insured versus uninsured versus underinsured; public versus private health plans; profit versus not-for-profit health plans), quality of physicians, regional variations in medical practices, and patient characteristics (such as clinical features of disease, or health literacy).

Of course, it is possible that both of these mechanisms—biased doctors and third factors—could operate simultaneously. Practical policymaking requires an inquiry into the relative contributions of each. In our view, it is the third factors that generate the strongest momentum in driving the differences between races in both care and outcomes. Indeed, for answers to the race-related differences in healthcare, it turns out that the doctor's office is not the most rewarding place to look. White and black patients, on average, do not even visit the same population of physicians—making the idea of preferential treatment by individual doctors a far less compelling explanation for disparities in health. Doctors whom black patients tend to see may not be in a position to provide optimal care. Furthermore, because healthcare varies a great deal depending on where people live, and because blacks are overrepresented in regions of the United States served by poorer healthcare facilities, disparities are destined to be, at least in part, a function of residence.

## IOM Report Asserts
## Discrimination the Cause

Yet the biased-doctor model has acquired considerable and unmerited weight in both academic literature and the popular press. It enjoyed a great boost in visibility from a 2002 report from the Institute of Medicine (IOM), part of the National Academy of Sciences, called *Unequal Treatment: Confronting Racial and Ethnic Disparities in Health Care.* The IOM provides lawmakers with advice on matters of biomedical science, medicine, and health, and issues high-profile reports written by panels of outside experts. *Unequal Treatment* was widely hailed as the authoritative study on health disparities. It concluded that the dynamics of the doctor-patient relationship—"bias," "prejudice," and "discrimination"—were a significant cause of the treatment differential and, by extension, of the poorer health of minorities.

Media fanfare greeted the IOM report in news stories bearing headlines like, "Color-Blind Care . . . Is Not What Minorities Are Getting" (*Newsday*); "Fed Report Cites 'Prejudice' in White, Minority Health Care Gap" (*Boston Herald*); and "Separate and Unequal" (*St. Louis Post-Dispatch*). Virtually every story ran the triumphant remark of Dr. Lucille Perez, then president of the National Medical Association, which represents black physicians: "It validates what many of us have been saying for so long—that racism is a major culprit in the mix of health disparities and has had a devastating impact on African-Americans."

There were a few dissenting voices. Among them was Richard Epstein, law professor at the University of Chicago. In his article "Disparities and Discrimination in Health Care Coverage: A Critique of the Institute of Medicine Study," he wrote:

> The IOM study adopts exactly the wrong approach. . . . Instead of dwelling [as the report does] on the Tuskegee experiments as evidence of current biases that linger within the system, I would trumpet the dedicated men and women in the profession who are determined to help people of all backgrounds and races deal with their health problems. . . . It is a shame to attack so many people of good will on evidence that admits a much more benign interpretation. . . . And there are enough problems in the healthcare system even without the genteel guilt trip that pervades the IOM study.

## Socioeconomic Status Predicts Health

Chronic disease, disability, and early death are destructive forces in individual lives and in whole communities. Their toll is high—and they do not strike at random. A growing body of evidence indicates that socioeconomic status (SES) is a strong predictor of health. Better health is associated with having more income, more years of education, and a more prestigious job, as well as living in neighborhoods where a higher percentage of residents have higher incomes and more education.

*The John D. and Catherine T. MacArthur Research Network on Socioeconomic Status and Health. www.macses.ucsf.edu.*

But Professor Epstein was drowned out by numerous commentators who implied or stated outright that current treatment differences are a product of a harsh racial climate and personal bias on the part of physicians. To read David Barton Smith, for example, one would think it was only yesterday, rather than forty years ago, that we stopped segregating hospitals and separating the blood supply by race. There "remain key parts of the unfinished civil rights agenda," writes the public policy expert at Temple University, pending "enough federal will and national unity" to resolve them.

In this monograph, we evaluate the studies routinely put forth as evidence of harmful discrimination. Because the IOM report represents the most popular synthesis of the disparities literature, we draw heavily on its analysis. We also examine evidence not considered by the IOM panel. These additional findings indicate that race-related variables, especially geography and socioeconomic status, shine important explanatory light into the recesses of the treatment gap.

## Race Matters Only Indirectly

We conclude that the studies examined by the IOM panel—consisting primarily of retrospective analyses of large health-system databases—fail to make a persuasive case that physician bias is a significant cause of disparate care or health status. In short, the studies fall short in trying to control for the wide array of factors that confound the influence of race on physicians' treatment decisions. Without adequate controls, it is simply not possible to distinguish care patterns that correlate with race from those that are due directly to race.

Indeed, as we will see, when researchers employ designs that control for more third factors, the magnitude of any race effect shrinks considerably, if it does not disappear altogether.

Furthermore, we challenge the validity of measures commonly used to quantify health disparities and to calibrate the success of efforts to improve minority health. (We refer here to the assessment of *relative* care—that is, measuring the ratio of procedures or other health services received by minorities compared with whites.) One reason we question these measures is that the fact that a group receives more services does not necessarily mean it will have better health outcomes. For example, whites often receive more invasive cardiac procedures than blacks, but among blacks and whites admitted with heart disease, the death rate for whites is not necessarily lower. Thus, if outcomes are the focus, blacks are not necessarily being undertreated. Instead, whites are perhaps being overtreated in some instances—given procedures that do not improve their prospects of surviving. Why might this be? It has been suggested that because whites are (or are perceived to be) more litigious, doctors practice defensive medicine with them. In addition, whites are more likely to be insured, so doctors have more incentive to order additional tests.

## Misplaced Focus

Second, the focus on relative differences masks absolute measures of improved care and thereby sends the wrong message to policymakers. For example, a 2004 study found that black patients with diabetes who attended a Bronx clinic were tested for diabetic control 53 percent of the time; whites were tested 57 percent of the time. This difference of four percentage points could be considered smaller (and better) than the testing differential of fourteen percentage points found at a Washington, D.C., clinic. But a further look shows that 59 percent of blacks in the Washington clinic were tested, versus 73 percent of whites. In absolute terms, the D.C. diabetics—both black and white—received better care than their Bronx counterparts, but a narrow judgment based on racial comparison alone suggests otherwise.

Indeed, absolute improvements in treatment—if they occur in all groups—will not close a gap. All boats will have risen, so to speak. The minority group will have gained significantly, and good news this surely is; but the measure of success is obscured if one fixates on relative measures. For example, after the Department of Health and Human Services (HHS) implemented three-year (1999–2002) locally based projects in each state to help underserved populations overcome "healthcare system and sociocultural barriers" to care, evaluators found they could not document a reduction in statewide disparities, in part because the health of whites improved along with those of minority groups. Although these projects were successful in improving overall community health, they failed to reduce racial disparities per se.

Conversely, a misplaced focus on narrowing of disparities can obscure deficiencies in care. Amal Trivedi and colleagues at Harvard, for example, found greater improvements in black patients than whites in receipt of required tests and treatments (for example, eye exams for diabetics or beta-blocker after heart attack) over a six-year period. The good news about the narrowed black-white differentials, however, was somewhat offset by the fact that neither white nor black patients, all of whom were enrolled in Medicare managed-care plans, received the tests with optimal regularity.

Unfortunately, many scholars who address the disparity problem neglect the bigger picture. As David Mechanic, a world authority on healthcare practices, laments, "Increasingly, much of the policy discussion is focused on whether disparities are increasing or decreasing and less so on which interventions can bring about the largest health gains for all." He points to black/white infant mortality ratios as an example. From 1980 to 2000, black infant deaths decreased by over one-third, but because white deaths decreased more, the ratio of black/white mortality actually increased.

"Simply focusing on ratios misses important advances," Mechanic writes, "and may confuse us as to what is and is not worth undertaking." In general, he points out, health conditions amenable to improvement through technology will inevitably benefit the most advantaged individuals and groups first because they have the knowledge, resources, and networks to gain access to them most quickly.

## Socioeconomic Status

This is a powerful illustration of how a narrow concentration on race distracts from the reality that the largest overall gain in population health comes from targeting disparities linked to socioeconomic class. True, race and class are intertwined and in some contexts can be proxies for one another, but they are both associated, independently, with health status. In fact, class makes a much greater contribution than race.

Consider the national data on mortality from heart disease. Adults in the bottom quarter of the income distribution are two to four times as likely to die from heart disease as those in the top quarter. The differences between blacks and whites are minor by comparison—the black death rate exceeds the white by only one-fifth. And middle-class blacks are much less vulnerable to fatal heart disease than low-income whites. Put another way, controlling for income, blacks have higher mortality than whites; but low-income blacks have more in common with low-income whites than with middle-class or wealthier blacks. Thus, the socioeconomic differences between racial groups are largely responsible for disparities in health status between whites and blacks.

## Focus Should Be on Improving Healthcare for All

The misplaced emphasis on relative care calls too much attention to the sensational but unsubstantiated idea that racial bias is a meaningful cause of health disparities. Not only is the charge of bias divisive, it siphons energy and resources from endeavors targeting system factors that are more relevant to improving minority health: expanding access to high-quality care and facilitating changes in individuals' lifestyles and their capacity to manage chronic disease. From this perspective, proposed race-based remedies for the treatment gap—such as racial preferences in admission to medical school, racial sensitivity training for doctors, and legal action using Title VI of the Civil Rights Act—become trivial or irrelevant at best, and potentially harmful at worst.

Given the enormous political emphasis on racial disparities, we are compelled to respond to those who see treatment differences through a racial lens and design healthcare policies accordingly. But a true public health solution to inadequate care—one that seeks to maximize the health of all Americans—would more properly target all underserved populations, irrespective of group membership. Success would be reflected in the improved health of these communities; and, because many of them happen to comprise large numbers of minorities, racial and ethnic care differentials would diminish as well.

> "Discrimination never comes at a good time, but to have it happen when you are sick and at your most vulnerable is absolutely devasting."

# Religiously Motivated Discrimination in Health Care Is Wrong

*Natalie Hope McDonald*

*In the following viewpoint, Natalie Hope McDonald reports for The Advocate, a national gay and lesbian news organization, that many states are considering legislation to allow doctors to practice religious discrimination. If state legislatures pass these laws, says McDonald, doctors could deny services to gays or lesbians or try to "cure" them of their homosexuality. McDonald asserts that religious discrimination could have devastating consequences for the health of homosexuals. McDonald is an editor and writer living in Philadelphia, PA.*

As you read, consider the following questions:

1. What happened to Guadelupe Benitez?

Natalie Hope McDonald, "The Hypocritical Oath: Come Out to Your Doctor, and You May Be Told to Go Elsewhere. Now Some Lawmakers Want to Legalize Religious Discrimination," *The Advocate*, April 11, 2006, pp. 42–43. Copyright © 2006 Liberation Publications, Inc. Reproduced by permission.

2. What proposal did Indiana state senator Patricia Miller put forward in 2005?

3. According to McDonald, what do many LGBT (lesbian, gay, bisexual, and transgender) people do when they feel betrayed by their doctor?

When Jamie Beiler went to a Florida doctor's office seeking treatment for bronchitis last year, she never imagined the staff would also try to cure her homosexuality. After she was examined by a physician's assistant, Beiler, 36, was handed a packet of materials from an organization that promises "reparative therapy" for gays and lesbians. "I felt like I had been violated," Beiler says. "To this day, I dread the thought of ever having to go to a doctor's office again."

## Many States Considering Conscientious Objector Policies

What happened to Belier is not uncommon. She recently filed a legal complaint—not a lawsuit, since it is apparently not yet possible to do so in the state of Florida—against the doctor, the state health department, and CIGNA Healthcare. In recent years [as of 2006], doctors and pharmacists across the country have been fighting for the right to incorporate their religion into their practice, often at the expense of gays and lesbians. And they are finding support in high places. Some judges have ruled in favor of the idea, and more than a dozen state legislatures are now considering bills that would allow medical professionals to refuse treatment to individuals based on religious and moral objections.

The "conscientious objector policy act," a bill that has been stalled in Michigan for several years, would attempt to give medical professionals the right to discriminate against LGBT people. "Ultimately, physicians would be able to refuse to provide medical care based on personal disapproval of [an individual's] sexual orientation," says Lois Uttley, director of the MergerWatch Project in New York City, a group that works to protect hospital-based services from being restricted by religiously sponsored health systems.

The legislative trend is part of the efforts by a conservative religious movement with increasing political clout, says Jennifer C. Pizer, senior counsel for the gay legal advocacy group Lambda Legal. "We have a lot of hard work ahead of us to persuade mainstream medical organizations, public health organizations, and other health policy experts to speak up forcefully in defense of LGBT patients," she says.

That happened in the case of Guadalupe Benitez, who was refused fertility treatment by the North Coast Women's Care Medical Group in Vista, Calif., in 1999, when Christine Brody, MD, cited religious objections in refusing to help Benitez and her partner, Joanne Clark, become parents. Benitez sued, and the California Medical Association (though not at first) eventually supported the claim that doctors should not have the right to discriminate on religious grounds.

A state appellate court didn't, though, ruling in December that doctors could argue in some circumstances that their "religious beliefs" prevent them from providing treatment; the court has, however, agreed to rehear the case and review new legal briefings. "They thought I would go away and not do anything," says Benitez, who after finding a new physician became a mother to a son, now 4, and eventually, twin girls. "But I'm doing this for everyone else."

## Religious Discrimination Illegal

Pizer, who is representing Benitez, says doctors who specialize in certain forms of treatment but refuse to provide that treatment to all patients risk running afoul of state and federal laws. "The right of religious liberty does not create a right to ignore laws that apply to everyone else," says Pizer. "Our Benitez case has shown that many health care professionals have been unaware that civil rights laws can apply to them."

# Only 35% of Gay Teens Tell Doctor Their Sexual Orientation

A survey of lesbian, gay and bisexual teenagers found that 70 percent said most people they knew were aware of their sexual orientation, but only 35 percent reported that their doctor knew, according to a new study by the RAND Corporation and UCLA.

The American Academy of Pediatrics, the American Medical Association and the Society for Adolescent Medicine all recommend that physicians discuss sexuality with all adolescents and provide nonjudgmental communication about sexual orientation. This is important because if a physician is aware of an adolescent patient's sexual orientation, the doctor can offer appropriate health education and counseling, identify individual risk, and perform targeted screening tests and treatment.

Dr. Garth D. Meckler, lead author of the study and an assistant professor of emergency medicine and pediatrics with the Oregon Health and Science University in Portland, Ore., said the survey results surprised researchers because the subjects were interviewed at an empowerment conference for lesbian, gay and bisexual youth.

"We knew that the sample that we chose was going to be a very 'out' sample," Meckler said. "We figured they would have a higher disclosure rate than most youth, and yet, despite being out to almost everyone in their lives, only 35 percent had told their doctor about their sexual orientation."

*RAND Corporation,*
*"Few Lesbian, Gay, Bisexual Teens Tell Their Doctor*
*Their Sexual Orientation, RAND Study Finds,"*
*news release, December 28, 2006. www.rand.org.*

But David Stevens, MD, executive director of the Christian Medical and Dental Associations in Bristol, Tenn., says civil rights should include allowing doctors to decide what is and is not in line with their own moral judgments. "An infertility specialist asked to assist in the creation of embryos for unmarried couples may violate the tenets of his or her religious beliefs," he says.

Some lawmakers agree. In 2005, Indiana state senator Patricia Miller put forth a proposal to bar unmarried couples, including gays and lesbians, from using medical procedures to conceive a child. Miller, a Republican from Indianapolis, eventually withdrew the measure but hasn't ruled out resurrecting it this year.

## Devastating Consequences

The growing presence of religious discrimination in medicine worries Kathleen DeBold, executive director of the Mautner Project, a national lesbian health organization in Washington D.C. "I am still shocked by the horror stories we hear from our clients," she says. One lesbian diagnosed with breast cancer received a packet of information that included a "virulently antigay comic book called *The Gay Blade*," says DeBold. Other lesbians have complained that when they came out, their doctors advised them to find another health care provider.

"Discrimination never comes at a good time, but to have it happen when you are sick and at your most vulnerable is absolutely devastating," says DeBold. "The doctor-patient relationship is based on trust. Having a provider judge and condemn us and prescribe homophobic reading materials is an abuse of power and complete betrayal of that trust. And that betrayal leads LGBT people to avoid or delay getting the healthcare we need—often with devastating consequences."

Matt Kraljev, 33, was afraid to come out to his longtime doctor. But after he was diagnosed with HIV and hepatitis C, the Philadelphia resident needed to talk about being gay. So he moved on to a doctor at Philadelphia's Mazzoni Center, a medical facility that specializes in caring for LGBT patients. "Many doctors just don't understand gay health care," he says. "I don't believe that straight doctors in general are aware of the ins and outs of taking care of gay men."

Kraljev's doctor, Robert Winn, says he is still surprised by the need for gay-specific treatment facilities. "I'd like to think in 2006 [homophobia] wouldn't be a problem," says Winn, who also serves as vice chair of the policy and advocacy committee for the Gay and Lesbian Medical Association. "But doctors are still saying, 'I can't take care of your kind.'"

In a big city like Philadelphia there are more options for gay patients, Winn says. But many of his patients end up at Mazzoni only after being turned away or finding unsatisfactory treatment at a hospital right down the street.

In addition to the obvious risks that medical discrimination imposes, there are emotional effects that can take an ongoing toll. Since Benitez was told by her doctor that she and her partner were not qualified to be parents, she has sought counseling. "It was very painful," she says. "I never thought I would encounter this. I never expected that my life would be exposed."

| "Congress should pass legislation to protect the consciences of individuals and businesses from the abortion and homosexual lobbies."

# Medical Professionals Should Be Free to Practice Religiously Motivated Discrimination

## Nedd Kareiva

*In the following viewpoint, Nedd Kareiva contends that people should not be forced to violate their consciences, and he admonishes the American Civil Liberties Union (ACLU) for trying to make conscientious objection illegal. Kareiva calls on the U.S. Congress to abolish hate crimes legislation and instead to adopt legislation protecting conscientious objectors and religious expression. Kareiva is the founder and director of the Stop the ACLU Coalition and a columnist for the grassroots organization Renew America.*

As you read, consider the following questions:

1. According to Kareiva, the ACLU has helped California, Oregon, and Illinois do what?

Nedd Kareiva, "Freedom of Conscience or Tyranny—Your Choice," Renew America, January 7, 2006. www.renewamerica.us. Copyright © 2006 by Nedd Kareiva. Reproduced by permission of the author.

2. The National Gay and Lesbian Task Force lists states with hate crime statutes. How many are based on gender identity?

3. According to Kareiva, what has been evident in ancient Roman civilization, as well as Canada, Sweden, Great Britain, and most of Europe?

Matters of conscience the ACLU [American Civil Liberties Union] and its ilk have litigated or are litigating to compel compliance against businesses or religious institutions:

- Lambda Legal, an ally of the ACLU, is appealing a ruling in favor of two doctors for refusing to perform artificial insemination on a California lesbian. The first round in court was in December of last year [2005].

- A California lawyer filed suit last month against a Lutheran school for dismissing two female students perceived to be lesbians by their actions [with] each other.

- The ACLU of New York is currently suing a Catholic school for firing an unmarried pregnant kindergarten teacher in October of last year.

- The ACLU of Washington state in 2004 successfully sued an online printer of wedding invitations for refusing to do a job for two homosexuals who were getting "married" in Canada. The suit put the owner, Patty Pauls, and her web site out of business, forced her to pay damages to one of the two plaintiffs and compelled her via Stalinist tactics to issue an apology, saying she will never discriminate against homosexuals again.

## Forcing Violations of Consciences

These are just a few examples of litigative tyranny imposed by the likes of the ACLU and other activist organizations to force violations of consciences on churches, religious schools and

## The Conscientious Objector Policy Act

Sec. 5. (1) A health care provider may assert as a matter of conscience an objection to providing or participating in a health care service that conflicts with his or her sincerely held religious or moral beliefs.

*Michigan State Senate, Committee on Health Policy, "The Conscientious Objector Policy Act," Bill 972 (2004).*

organizations and businesses run by morally minded individuals. The ACLU is one group that loves touting the "principle" of keeping religion and government apart (the so-called separation of church and state doctrine found nowhere in the Constitution) but is certainly ready to call down the power of the government on those opposed to its agenda if it can exploit a law on the books.

The ACLU has helped states like California, Oregon and Illinois craft legislation to prevent churches and religious businesses from firing or refusing to hire homosexuals, transsexuals and transvestites (cross-dressers for the politically correct). In California, it can cost business owners, Christian or not, up to $150,000 if he or she fires a cross-dresser in his or her ranks.

When businesses can't make decisions based on the consciences of its owners but have to surrender their values to laws liberals helped put on the books based on certain euphemisms to make them sound nice (e.g. equality, non-discrimination, fairness, privacy), we have a serious problem on our hands. Forcing pharmacists and hospitals to issue contraceptives, forcing business owners and religious institutions to cater to sexual preferences and practices they oppose and even forcing landlords of office and apartment buildings to acquiesce to such behaviors is not only un-American, it is Communist in nature and origin (like the ACLU).

# Hate Crimes Legislation Promotes Culture of Perversion

Congress passed legislation which was signed last year [in 2005] by President Bush to allow doctors and hospitals to opt [out] of doing or referring to abortions, a law currently challenged by the state of California. Unfortunately, while Congress has diligently worked to promote a pro-life culture by passing bills to that effect, they have at the same time worked to promote a culture of perversion by promoting hate crimes legislation based on sexual preferences.

The House, having rejected revising hate crimes law in previous Congresses, passed such a bill last year. Fortunately, while having passed it in previous legislative terms, the U.S. Senate thus far has not taken a vote on it. Hate crimes legislation is bad for America and resolves little, if anything, by their existence other than promote protection based on sexual behaviors.

Our nation is inundated with hundreds of thousands of laws on the book from virtually anything imaginable. Many of these laws are totally useless, unenforceable and unnecessary. When a new law is signed into being, it means more money and resources to enforce it. A vast majority of them should not be given the time nor day. But given the nature of attacks on businesses and religious institutions who wish to retain moral standards, legislation is sorely needed to address the conscience vs. tyranny war.

Congress could first start by not only scrapping laws based on sexual preferences and identity but unilaterally banning federal hate crimes laws, period, since such violate the equal protection of the 14th Amendment. This would appear on the surface to infringe on states' rights but because there has been wide disparities of applications as well as abuse from state to state on these issues, a uniform policy would seem to be in order and could be crafted without violating the Constitution.

The National Gay & Lesbian Task Force lists 29 states having hate crimes statutes which include sexual orientation, including 7 based on gender identity, meaning whatever sex or gender one individual perceives him or herself to be. Such laws are wrong since they single out classes of people based on sexual activity. They should be abolished on the basis of the 14th Amendment.

## Protect Conscientious Objectors

Next, Congress should pass legislation to protect the consciences of individuals and businesses from the abortion and homosexual lobbies. Such legislation also could potentially be prone to abuse and open up many cans of worms. But it need not be that way if carefully crafted towards the individual and the business, church or religious organization more so than the issue.

Despite certain polls showing more young people in support of same sex marriage and civil unions now than a decade or two ago, there are still substantial numbers of Americans who oppose them as shown by the number of states that have passed marriage amendments. Many of these traditional marriage supporters are live and let live and will even hire such individuals, provided their lifestyles are not shoved in their faces while on the job. They should be protected.

Similar numbers show the promotion of abortion to be declining and more and more Americans, while not necessarily wanting to toss *Roe vs. Wade*, support greater restrictions of it.

Now am I suggesting that homosexuals, transsexuals and transvestites be tossed out on the streets? Hardly. No such epidemic exists today anyway. But I do suggest individuals who purchase the apartment buildings, fix them up to be rented out, undergo inspections to make sure their edifices are sound, start the businesses, pay the costs to get them started and the taxes to keep them going and endure all the regulations imposed on them have their say so on who prospective tenants and employees shall and shall not be, not the government or the likes of the ACLU.

## Protect Religious Expression

When a nation's acknowledgement of God and its religious heritage take a back seat and succumb to the forces of secularism through nicely worded euphemisms and when such forces are compressed on our businesses, churches and religious institutions, the nation's greatness starts to go. This has been evident throughout the ages from ancient Roman civilization to the current decline of otherwise technologically advanced countries like Canada, Sweden, Great Britain as well as most of Europe. Items creating this state of decadence include the virtual unrestricted practice of abortion, promotion of homosexual marriages, civil unions, adoptions, hate crimes laws, unlimited free marketing of pornography and governments refusing to recognize God.

America is known throughout the globe military-wise as the world's superpower. However, at the rate our country is going, it's superpower status morally is entering free fall. America must protect religious expression on the businesses, churches and religious organizations that wish to uphold it and do so now. If we allow the previous examples of euphemisms to continue superseding our religious values and conscience and taking hold on our moral infrastructure, we will eviscerate quickly and become invisible like the aforementioned countries are.

The question is can we afford to go there. Tyranny is sure to be found if we do. And if we do, I would wager (though I'm not a betting man) it will likely be permanent. We've already well past the starting gate. I'd say we're halfway to the "finish line" now, perhaps more than halfway.

Anyone want to take me up on my "offer"?

# Periodical Bibliography

*The following articles have been selected to supplement the diverse views presented in this chapter.*

Brietta R. Clark
"Hospital Flight from Minority Communities: How Our Existing Civil Rights Framework Fosters Racial Inequality in Healthcare," *DePaul Journal of Health Care Law*, Spring 2006.

Michelle Chen
"Housing Watchdogs Call Post-Katrina Ordinance 'Racist,'" *New Standard*, October 6, 2006.

Margaret Chon and Donna E. Arzt
"Walking While Muslim," *Law and Contemporary Problems*, Spring 2005.

Kirstin Downey
"Segregation Persists In Housing, Study Says," *Washington Post*, April 6, 2005.

Malcolm Gladwell
"Troublemakers: What Pit Bulls Can Teach Us About Profiling," *New Yorker*, February 6, 2006.

Dina M. Horwedel
"Opening Eyes and Minds: As Americans' Perceptions of Islam Grow Increasingly Negative, Muslim Students and Professors Find Themselves Educating Their College Communities," *Diverse: Issues in Higher Education*, May 18, 2006.

Jennifer LaFleur
"Black Wealth Blossoms in Suburbs," *Dallas Morning News*, June 25, 2005.

Michael Nowicki
"Poor Management Can Look Like Discrimination," *Healthcare Financial Management*, April 2006.

Kai Wright
"What Your Doctor Won't See . . . If Conservatives Make Healthcare Colorblind," *Colorlines Magazine*, March–April 2007.

OPPOSING
VIEWPOINTS®
SERIES

CHAPTER 3

# Is Affirmative Action an Effective Remedy for Discrimination?

# Chapter Preface

"As a twenty-three-year-old recent college graduate, now current graduate student," writes Cristina Viray in the Diversity Training Group (DTG) Web site, "I represent a growing population unique to my generation, coming from a racially mixed background (in my case, Filipino, Italian, and Polish). I am generation Y (born immediately after Generation X, the last generation wholly born in the 20th century). I am one of approximately 76 million people in this country changing both the face and the focus of today's workplace. My generation rivals the baby boomer generation in size and is the most racially diverse in the history of the United States." Cristina is a summer associate at DTG, a company that provides diversity training to government agencies and businesses. Diversity has been used to make the case for affirmative action and other programs that attempt to remedy discrimination; however, some people think that diversity promotes racism.

Many American universities, businesses, and governmental agencies have diversity as a goal. Believing that their organizations should reflect the racial, ethnic, and cultural make up of the country, institutions such as the University of Michigan, businesses such as Microsoft, and government agencies like the U.S. Coast Guard may use diversity goals in their admission or hiring processes. They also may contract with providers of diversity training, such as DTG, to teach diversity to their current workforce. The goal of diversity training is to help people of different cultures, races, ethnicities, sexual orientation, religions, and genders to learn about each other, to accept, tolerate, and even embrace their differences, so as to be able to work together in the most efficient manner. John DiBiaggio, former president of Tufts University, Michigan State University, and the University of Connecticut, has said that diversity is important for three fundamental reasons: "First, encouraging and fostering, within our community, a blending of ethnicities, cultures, races, religions, and genders is educationally sound. It is our obligation to prepare our students to live and work in a highly diverse society. . . . Second, diversity should be realized at Tufts and elsewhere for moral reasons." We have a responsibility, he continues, to "address the vestiges of past racial injustices and to confront those that persist today. . . . Finally, the practical implications [of diversity] speak for themselves. . . . To deny quality educational opportunities to the fastest growing segment of our population simply does not make good business sense."

Nonetheless, many people believe when organizations seek diversity they are being racist. Peter Schwartz of the Ayn Rand Institute said the following about diversity and racism: "They [those who favor diversity programs] imply that people have worthwhile views to express because of their ethnicity, and that 'diversity' enables us to encounter 'black ideas,' 'Hispanic ideas,' etc. What could be more repulsively racist than that? This is exactly the premise held by the South's slave-owners and by the Nazis' Storm Troopers. They too believed that an individual's thoughts and actions are determined by his racial heritage." Columnist Jan Larson has stated that diversity goals present a conundrum and can lead to racism. Writing in the *American Chronicle*, Larson said, "It isn't surprising that many people cannot make the distinction between racism to be reviled versus diversity to be embraced. On one hand, we must appreciate our differences to be diverse, but on the other hand, we must all be alike to avoid racism. While diversity is not something to be avoided, it cannot be forced, as with affirmative action programs, or it leads to division, resentment and yes, racism."

Some people and organizations think diversity is a noble goal and a remedy to racism and discrimination, while other people and groups hold the opposite sentiment. They think that seeking diversity is a racist act since it considers people different *because of* their race, ethnicity, or culture.

The contributors of the viewpoints in the following chapter offer opposing viewpoints on affirmative action and whether it is an effective way to remedy discrimination.

| "Simply put, affirmative action works. Students and faculty of all races have considered it an important part of their education and preparation for adulthood in an increasingly diverse nation."

# Affirmative-Action Programs Are Necessary

*Gary Orfield*

*In this viewpoint, Gary Orfield contends that the U.S. Supreme Court's decision in the University of Michigan affirmative action case was right: college admissions policies that value diversity, such as affirmative action programs, are necessary and important for the nation. Orfield asserts that schools and communities across the country are deeply divided, with whites increasingly being isolated from blacks and other racial groups. But the nation and the world are comprised of diverse racial and ethnic groups and diversity on college campuses is important for the success of future leaders in our nation. Orfield is professor of education and social policy at the Harvard Graduate School of Education.*

Gary Orfield, "Preserving Diversity: The Supreme Court's Affirmative Action," *Ed. Magazine*, Harvard Graduate School of Education, July 1, 2004. www.gse.harvard.edu. Copyright © 2007 President and Fellows of Harvard College. Reproduced by permission.

As you read, consider the following questions:

1. What percentage of law students at the University of Michigan reported that diversity had a positive impact on how they think and learn about legal issues?

2. According to Orfield, affirmative action opponents wanted to ban the use of race as a factor in admitting students but leave other factors in place. What were those factors?

3. In 1954, minorities comprised what percentage of students in U.S. public schools?

As a believer in vigorous civil discourse, I challenge conservative critics who have harshly attacked the Supreme Court's decision in June 2003 in the University of Michigan affirmative action case, claiming that it will divide America. Justice Sandra Day O'Connor, in particular, was assailed for citing, in her majority opinion, social-science research that demonstrates the value of diversity. Affirmative action opponents wanted the case decided on the basis of their preferred legal doctrine of "colorblindness," not on research findings about results. Several HGSE [Harvard Graduate School of Education] researchers, including two doctoral students, contributed to the studies that were relied on in the Court's ruling and in the concurring opinion signed by Justices Ginsburg and Breyer. I am very proud that Harvard made a major contribution to the decision to uphold affirmative action; this was probably the most important civil rights decision in a generation.

## Schools Divided and Unequal

Census data and school statistics reveal that in spite of the progress made during the civil rights era, our communities and schools are deeply divided and increasingly unequal. Whites now account for only three in five U.S. students but are highly isolated. Our study, *A Multiracial Society with Seg-*

*regated Schools*, cited in two court opinions, reports that due to the dismantling of desegregation plans, students are now more segregated—by race and by income—than they have been since the 1960s.

Students in segregated schools typically perform considerably worse on test scores partly because 90 percent of highly segregated minority schools confront the problems and inequalities poor families and communities face. Since the mid-1980s, the achievement gap, which had narrowed during the 1970s and early 1980s, started to grow again as schools became more segregated and economic inequality grew in the society.

## Students Appreciate Diversity

Research also demonstrates that students of all races strongly appreciate the opportunity to learn in diverse settings. The Court referred to findings of a survey of law students at the University of Michigan and at Harvard (which I conducted with Dean Whitla, HGSE lecturer on education) that found that 89 to 91 percent of the students reported that diversity had a positive impact on how they learn and think about legal issues. Nearly two-thirds of the students surveyed reported that diversity improved classroom discussion and also enhanced their ability to work more effectively and/or get along better with others. The students also reported that diverse classrooms often changed their views of criminal justice, civil rights, and the role of their profession.

## College Admissions Best Left to Faculty

The Supreme Court's decision recognized the historic tradition of letting college faculties make judgments about admissions themselves. Virtually every selective university in the country supported this decision. Affirmative action opponents wanted the Supreme Court to override the judgment of faculties across the country and forbid using race as a factor in admitting students, all the while leaving intact a huge range of special considerations given to children of alumni, donors, athletes, students from particular states, and many other preferences at various colleges and universities. Is it fair to favor students who score slightly higher on standardized tests because their parents were able to afford test prep courses or expensive suburban homes in communities with quality schools? Banning affirmative action would have excluded "minorities"—who now make up the majority of the school-age children in a growing number of states—from remaining a significant presence at their flagship state universities. The ruling did not divide an integrated nation; it was an attempt to integrate a divided nation.

Despite the "liberal" characterization of the Court's decision, the case's outcome was actually conservative in one important respect: it supports the way that college and university admissions have been conducted since the 1960s.

## Our Schools and Our Nation Are Diverse

If our institutions are to endure, they must open up to include those who have been historically excluded, because the stakes are rising. The demographics of our nation have changed massively in the past 40 years. When the Supreme Court outlawed segregation in 1954, U.S. public schools were comprised of approximately 12 percent minority students. Today, our nation's public schools are comprised of nearly 40 percent minorities. Within a generation, if existing trends continue, American schools will no longer have a European-American majority.

Affirmative action is not just about legal rights; it puts to use the great strength of our national identity: diversity. How can the rising ranks of leaders in education, politics, and business continue to fully succeed without the roots of a common educational experience? How can they understand the world in which they live and seek to lead, if they become increasingly divorced from the fastest-growing segments of our population? This is precisely the reason why topflight corporation and military leaders joined university administrators in supporting affirmative action before the Supreme Court. Justice O'Connor is a strong Conservative on most issues. In the Court's decision, she wrote: "We have repeatedly acknowledged the overriding importance of preparing students for work and citizenship, describing education as pivotal to 'sustaining our political and cultural heritage' with a fundamental role in maintaining the fabric of society." She went on to write that citizens of every race and class must be included to realize the dream of becoming "one nation, indivisible."

## Affirmative Action Is Important

Simply put, affirmative action works. Students and faculty of all races have considered it an important part of their education and preparation for adulthood in an increasingly diverse nation. Those of us who worked on this issue in the Civil Rights Project were proud to have collaborated with scholars across the country in developing evidence that helped the Supreme Court understand the vital successes of multiracial colleges. That kind of diversity is something we are fortunate to experience daily at HGSE. With affirmative action secure for our time, we must get busy doing the serious work needed to make better use of the important possibilities it provides.

"There are few ideals that are more fundamental to the definition of America
than equality. But this ideal is constantly being trampled in the service of
'diversity.'"

# Affirmative-Action Programs Are Unnecessary and Discriminatory

*Ward Connerly*

*In this viewpoint, Ward Connerly asserts that affirmative action
programs are discriminatory and go against American ideals of
equality. Connerly says affirmative action, with its attendant
goal of diversity, is really a quota system. He implores people to
support state initiatives, such as the Michigan Civil Rights Initiative (MCRI), that seek to ban affirmative action (the MCRI
was approved by Michigan voters in November 2006). Connerly,
nationally known as an outspoken opponent of affirmative action, is an author and former member of the University of California Board of Regents.*

As you read, consider the following questions:

1. What does the 1964 Civil Rights Act demand?

Ward Connerly, "The Road to Equality: The Michigan Civil Rights Initiative," *FlashRe-
port*, January 9, 2006. www.flashreport.org. Reproduced by permission.

2. California's Proposition 209 was also called what?

3. What did the U.S. Supreme Court say about diversity in its 2003 decision involving Gratz and Grutter?

Most Americans believe that discrimination based on the color of an individual's skin, or that person's gender, or the origin of one's ancestors, or a person's ethnic background or "race," is wrong. We have arrived at this belief as a result of a tumultuous period in American history, and because there is something about the character of the American people that places high value on the concept of fairness. "Do unto others as you would have them do unto you" is the centerpiece of the value system that we teach our children.

## Reverse Discrimination

We expect our government to conduct itself according to this value and to treat each of us impartially and equally. Favoritism based on the factors mentioned above is obnoxious to most Americans. During the last quarter of the 20th Century, American Institutions began to embrace discrimination—as long as it isn't against what we call "people of color." Moreover, the practice of applying different standards in college admissions and setting aside contracts for "minorities" and women is never called discrimination, when it is to the benefit of such individuals. Instead, such practices are called "affirmative action" or the promotion of "diversity."

It is widely believed that the problem of racial discrimination was solved, at least in a legal sense, in 1964, when the Congress enacted and President Lyndon Baines Johnson signed the 1964 Civil Rights Act. That act commands all government institutions to treat Americans as equals, without regard to their race, color or ethnic background or gender.

## States Act to Ban Affirmative Action

Unfortunately, the ink on the 1964 Civil Rights Act wasn't even dry before race advocates began to ignore it and to demand preferential treatment for "minorities." Toward the end of the 20th Century, many Americans began to challenge policies and practices that promoted racial discrimination. In California, that challenge came in the form of a resolution approved by the Regents of the University of California (1995) prohibiting race preferences, and a ballot proposition authored by Glynn Custred and Tom Wood that was appropriately named the "California Civil Rights Initiative" (CCRI). CCRI (Proposition 209) was decisively approved by the California electorate in 1996. I am proud to have been the chairman of the 209 campaign and to have conceived and led the action adopted by the Regents.

In 1998, by an overwhelming margin of 59-41, the people of the State of Washington approved an Initiative (I-200) patterned after Prop. 209. Once again, I had the pleasure of playing a significant role in that election. Two years later, Governor Jeb Bush signed an Executive Order, "One Florida," that was intended to preempt the "Florida Civil Rights Initiative," which many of us were seeking to place before the voters of that state.

Ballot initiatives weren't the only device being used to challenge race discrimination. During the decade of the 1990s, lawsuits were also becoming more common. Two suits were filed by Jennifer Gratz and Barbara Grutter, both of whom had been denied admission to the undergraduate school and the law school, respectively, of the University of Michigan. Both suits challenged the use of race preferences in college admissions, with the overarching question being: Is the pursuit of "diversity" a compelling justification for the use of race preferences?

## University of Michigan

On June 23, 2003, the United States Supreme Court handed down its decision involving Gratz and Grutter. While many of

## Fighting Affirmative Action in Michigan

In Michigan, it's Ward Connerly and Jennifer Gratz versus the state's entire political establishment—and Gratz and Connerly may actually win. Connerly, an African-American businessman famous for being the force behind affirmative action bans that passed in California and Washington in the late 1990s, is now pushing his favorite cause in Michigan. A group he helped found called the Michigan Civil Rights Initiative is backing an initiative on the state's ballot in November that would ban both racial and gender preferences in state government hiring and college admissions. Gratz, who after being denied admission to the University of Michigan filed suit in a case that eventually reached the Supreme Court, is leading the effort. The forces opposing them are vast and cover the entire political spectrum: the Democratic and Republican candidates for governor in Michigan, labor unions like the United Auto Workers, top officials at two of the state's biggest businesses, Ford and General Motors, the Chamber of Commerce groups in several of the state's cities and the Michigan Catholic Conference, as well as national groups like the NAACP [National Association for the Advancement of Colored People] and the Urban League. "It's a very lonely battle," Connerly told *Time* earlier this year.

*Perry Bacon Jr., "Campaign '06:*
*A Fight Over Affirmative Action in Michigan,"*
*Time, October 26, 2006. www.time.com.*

those who sought an end to race preferences and discrimination had banked their hopes on a court decision in favor of equal treatment for every person, the Court ruled otherwise. In a muddled ruling, with Justice Sandra Day O'Connor casting the decisive vote in a 5-4 decision, the Court legally sanctioned race preferences and deemed "diversity" to be a compelling objective.

The Court acknowledged, however, that the granting of race preferences was undesirable, in the long run. In her majority opinion, Justice O'Connor expressed the aspiration that in 25 years "race preferences" would no longer be necessary. In addition, the Court noted the passage of Proposition 209 in California and I-200 in Washington as examples of States where race-blind approaches had been approved. The Court gave its nod of the head to race-blind policies as a preferred approach.

Shortly after the Court decision, I received a call from Jennifer Gratz seeking my help to place an initiative on the ballot in Michigan that would be patterned after Proposition 209. After considerable thought (five minutes), I decided that Michigan would become our new battleground to get the government out of the business of playing race favorites. . . .

## Diversity Means Quotas

There are few ideals that are more fundamental to the definition of America than equality. But this ideal is constantly being trampled in the service of "diversity." The pursuit of "diversity" has become a compelling reason to discriminate, as long as the perceived beneficiaries are women and "minorities." The rationale for this new religion of "diversity" is that America is a better place when all of our institutions are "diverse." And, because "diversity" is regarded as such a redeeming value, it is essentially acceptable to a frightening number of Americans that "diversity" be pursued and achieved "by any means necessary."

Yet, there is not one major American success throughout our history that can be attributed to "diversity." All that we are as a nation we owe to merit and individual enterprise. "Diversity" is little more than quotas in drag; and a quota system is the antithesis of a meritocracy. Quotas seek to build a workforce, a student body, a team, that "looks like America," or that "reflects the ethnic and racial composition of the community." An enterprise or venue based on merit simply tries to be the best that it can be with nary a thought given to the physical or ancestral characteristics of those involved.

A quota is not just a fixed number. It is the effort to engineer the outcome of a competitive process and to achieve proportionality based on group identity. Quotas rely on the principle of group representation. "Critical mass" and "diversity" are nothing more than euphemisms for the word "quotas." Any effort to subordinate the operation of the meritocratic principle is an effort to achieve a quota.

## Michigan Civil Rights Initiative

It is the purpose of the Michigan Civil Rights Initiative (MCRI) to challenge the notion that the governmental pursuit of "diversity" should be triumphant over the principles of individual merit and "equal treatment under the law for every person."

MCRI would install language in the Michigan constitution preventing "the state from discriminating against, or granting preferential treatment to, any individual or group on the basis of race, color, gender, ethnicity or national origin in public employment, public education, or public contracting."

If we are to cleanse our nation of this quota poison, it is critical that we consciously grab hold of the principle of merit and embrace a single standard for all in the private, public, nonprofit, and philanthropic sectors of our society.

Throughout the nation, all of those who embrace this approach of fairness and equality should lend their support to the Michigan Civil Rights Initiative.

*"Blacks are the victims of law school programs of affirmative action, not the beneficiaries."*

# Race-Based Affirmative Action Hurts African Americans

### Richard H. Sander

*In this viewpoint, Richard H. Sander argues that affirmative action programs at the nation's law schools are counter-productive; they hurt blacks more than they help them. Sander used 2001 law school admissions data and other information to get a picture of the complete legal education system. He concludes that blacks are directly hurt by affirmative action and racial preferences—without affirmative action more blacks would become lawyers—and indirectly hurt by the stigma of preferences and the impact of low grades on self-esteem. Sander claims the benefits of affirmative action for blacks are minor compared to the costs. Sander is a professor of law at the University of California, Los Angeles (UCLA).*

As you read, consider the following questions:

1. According to Sander, what are the two primary benefits of affirmative action?

Richard H. Sander, "A Systematic Analysis of Affirmative Action in American Law Schools," *Stanford Law Review*, November 2004, vol. 57, no. 2, pp. 478–82.

2. Historically, when did U.S. law schools begin to actively seek to increase black enrollment?

3. Justice O'Connor's decision in the *Grutter* case draws heavily on amicus briefs that paint what kind of picture of affirmative action?

I began this article with a simple question: does affirmative action, as practiced by American law schools, clearly help blacks more than it hurts them? Although I started this project with serious doubts about some things law schools were doing, the answer to the big question turned out to be far less ambiguous than I would have imagined possible. Law school admissions preferences impose enormous costs on blacks and create relatively minor benefits. By looking at law schools systemically, we can see patterns and larger consequences that would be invisible or speculative if we looked at any one school or group of schools in isolation. As it is, the key features of the current system seem very clear.

## Costs Outweigh Benefits

For blacks, there are two primary benefits of affirmative action. First, black students widely have the opportunity to attend significantly more elite schools than do white peers with similar credentials. Preferences boost students up the hierarchy of 184 schools by 20 to 50 steps, sometimes more; a very large majority of black students accept these opportunities and attend schools that used preferences to admit them. Second, the system as a whole leads to the admission of an additional five or six hundred black students—about one-seventh of the annual total—who would not otherwise be admitted to any accredited school. Cutting against these benefits are six major costs of the current system of racial preferences.

1. *Black students as a whole are at a substantial academic disadvantage when they attend schools that used preferences to admit them.* As a consequence, they perform

poorly as a group throughout law school. The median GPA of all black students at the end of the first year of law school lies roughly at the sixth percentile of the white grade distribution. Put differently, close to half of black students end up in the bottom tenth of their classes. This performance gap is entirely attributable to preferences; none of it seems to be attributable to race per se.

2. *The clustering of black students near the bottom of the grade distribution produces substantially higher attrition rates.* Entering black law students are 135% more likely than white students to not get a law degree. Part of this is the effect of low grades on academically strong black students who would have easily graduated from less competitive schools; part of this is the effect of high attrition among the five or six hundred academically weak black students admitted to the low-prestige law schools. But again, virtually all of the black-white gap seems attributable to preferences; virtually none of it seems attributable to race or to any correlate of race (such as income).

3. *Generally low grades among blacks have even larger effects on bar performance.* Blacks are nearly six times as likely as whites to not pass state bar exams after multiple attempts. The difference, again, is mostly attributable to preferences. Half of the black-white bar passage gap is traceable to the effects of blacks with good credentials getting low grades at higher-prestige schools; nearly a quarter is due to low-prestige schools admitting blacks with lower credentials than almost any of the other students in the system.

4. *When blacks pass the bar and enter the job market, they encounter a generally positive climate.* Blacks earn 6% to 9% more early in their careers than do whites seeking similar jobs with similar credentials, presumably because

many employers (including government employers) pursue moderate racial preferences in hiring. Nonetheless, affirmative action by schools hurts blacks in the job market more than it helps. The data suggests that employers weigh law school grades far more heavily in evaluating job candidates than most legal academics have assumed. Law school racial preferences give blacks fancier degrees, but also systematically lower their GPAs. For at least two-thirds of black law graduates, the harm preferences do to a student's grades greatly outweighs the benefit derived from the more prestigious degree. Only black students graduating from the top ten law schools even arguably derive net benefits from this trade-off. Racial preferences therefore have not been an indispensable part of credentialing blacks for the job market; overall, they clearly end up shutting more doors than they open.

5. *In 2001, about 86% of all black students who attended accredited American law schools would have been eligible for admission at one or more law schools in the total absence of racial preferences.* System-wide, racial preferences expand the pool of blacks in law school by only 14%. These 14%—about five to six hundred students admitted to low-prestige schools—have very low academic credentials and face long odds against becoming lawyers. Only a fifth of this group finishes law school and passes the bar on their first attempt; fewer than a third become lawyers after multiple attempts at taking the bar.

6. *When one takes into account the corrosive effects of racial preferences on the chances of all black law students to graduate and pass the bar, these preferences probably tend, system-wide, to shrink rather than expand the total number of new black lawyers each year.* If all preferences were abolished, the data suggests that the number of black attorneys emerging from the class of 2004 would be 7%

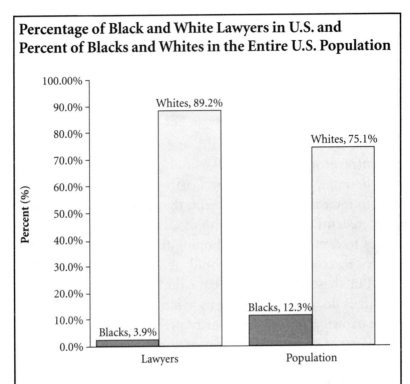

**Percentage of Black and White Lawyers in U.S. and Percent of Blacks and Whites in the Entire U.S. Population**

TAKEN FROM: Commission on Racial and Ethnic Diversity in the Profession, American Bar Association. Based on 2000 Census Data, U.S. Census Bureau.

larger than it is. The number of black attorneys passing the bar on their first attempt would be 20% larger. These numbers are simply estimates, resting on the assumptions I have detailed; but even if the attrition effects of the current system were much smaller than I have estimated, we would still be producing approximately the same number—and much better trained—black attorneys under a race-blind system.

## Stigma of Preferences

These are simply the direct, easily quantifiable effects of law school racial preferences. I have said nothing about the stigma of preferences, about the effect of low grades on student esteem, about the life consequences for hundreds of young blacks each year who invest years of effort and thousands in expense but never become lawyers, or about the loss to communities that could be served by black lawyers but are not because racial preferences have had the effect in recent years of reducing our annual output of qualified black attorneys.

There are many ironies in this state of affairs, but perhaps the central irony is this: Law schools adopted racial preferences because, soon after they began to seek actively in the 1960s to increase black enrollment, they confronted the black-white credentials gap. The schools conceived of preferential policies to overcome the gap, hoping that by ignoring the differences in credentials they could perhaps make the gap go away. But these very policies have the effect of widening the credentials disadvantage facing individual black students rather than narrowing it. The effect of preferences on black graduation rates is similar to the effect of subtracting 60-odd points from the academic index of every black matriculant. The effect of preferences on black bar passage rates is similar to the effect of subtracting 120 points. Large-scale preferences exacerbate the problems they try, cosmetically, to cover up.

## Law School Conduct

What can be said about the conduct of law schools in this system? Looking back over the years of the rise and development of the modern system of racial preferences, I think it is fair to say that there was a good deal of honor in what law schools did during the first ten years of this era. From the late 1960s through the time of *Bakke* [the landmark 1978 affirmative action case], law schools shook off their complacency as overwhelmingly white bastions of prestige. They critically examined old procedures, experimented with new admissions methods, and sponsored summer programs like CLEO [the Council on Legal Education Opportunity] that worked hard to broaden and deepen the field of potential minority students. Reports from that period are infused with a degree of honesty and openness. And these policies did transform the image of law school and increased the interest of young minority college students in making law school a goal.

The era since *Bakke* has been quite different. Schools have felt hemmed in. The cascade effect of preferences exercised by law schools as a whole meant that any individual school had to choose between either having only a handful of black students or preserving racially segregated admissions procedures. Pressures from students and faculty, and fears of appearing racist, made this seem to be no choice at all. *Bakke* provided a convenient veil of diversity that could be draped over policies that were substantively hard to distinguish from those the Supreme Court had struck down. Viewing [Supreme Court Justice Lewis F.] Powell's holding as hypocritical, law school deans joined in the hypocrisy. For most, this probably seemed a small price to pay in the cause of an apparently greater good.

Unfortunately, once law schools had adopted the pretense that students of all races at any institution had essentially the same qualifications, it was difficult for anyone to pursue serious research into the effects of affirmative action, or even for faculties to engage in honest discussion. The entire topic has been largely given over to myth-making and anecdote for an entire generation. It should perhaps not be so surprising, then, that a close look at the emperor today shows such an unflattering nakedness.

## University of Michigan's Decisions Based on False Premises

What are the implications of this analysis for the law of affirmative action? There are three. First, the distinction drawn by Justice O'Connor between the admissions systems of the University of Michigan's law school and its undergraduate college is a false one. It is impossible to explain the admissions outcomes at the law school, or at any other law school we have examined, unless the schools are either adding points to the academic indices of blacks or separating admissions decisions into racially segregated pools.

Second, Justice O'Connor's decision in *Grutter* is wrong in a broader sense. Her opinion draws heavily on amicus briefs that paint a glowing picture of the benefits of affirmative action and its indispensability as a vehicle of mobility by blacks into the legal profession. The premise accepted by O'Connor is that racial preferences are indispensable to keep a reasonable number of blacks entering the law and reaching its highest ranks—a goal which is in turn indispensable to a legitimate and moral social system. The analysis in this Article demonstrates that this premise is wrong. Racial preferences in law schools, at least as applied to blacks, work against all of the goals that O'Connor held to be important. The conventional wisdom about these preferences is invalid.

## Affirmative Action Hurts Blacks

But a third legal implication of this work is the most important of all. All of the Supreme Court's decisions about affirmative action in higher education presume that the discrimination involved is fundamentally benign. It is tolerable only because it operates on behalf of a politically vulnerable minority—that is, blacks. A preferences program that operated on behalf of whites would be unconstitutional beyond question.

Yet if the findings in this Article are correct, blacks are the victims of law school programs of affirmative action, not the beneficiaries. The programs set blacks up for failure in school, aggravate attrition rates, turn the bar exam into a major hurdle, disadvantage most blacks in the job market, and depress the overall production of black lawyers. Whites, in contrast, arguably benefit from preferences in a number of ways. Whites have higher grades because blacks and other affirmative action beneficiaries fill most of the lower ranks; whites are the most obvious beneficiaries of the diversity produced by affirmative action programs; it is even plausible to argue that bar passage rates are kept high to avoid embarrassingly high failure rates by minority exam-takers. The next legal challenge to affirmative action practices by law schools could very plausibly be led by black plaintiffs who were admitted, spent years and thousands of dollars on their educations, and then never passed the bar and never became lawyers—all because of the misleading double standards used by law schools to admit them, and the schools' failure to disclose to them the uniquely long odds against their becoming lawyers. And these plaintiffs, unlike the plaintiffs in *Hopwood* and *Gratz*, could be entitled to more than nominal damages.

> "We believe that the effect of cutting out about three fourths of the African American students at the country's most highly regarded law schools would harm not only African Americans seeking to be lawyers but also white students and the nation as a whole."

# Race-Based Affirmative Action Has Helped African Americans

*David L. Chambers, Timothy T. Clydesdale, William C. Kidder, and Richard O. Lempert*

*In this viewpoint, the authors contend that affirmative action programs provide more benefits than costs to African Americans and the nation as a whole. They refute and pick apart an opposing argument proposed by Richard H. Sander that affirmative action programs hurt more than they help. The authors contend that without affirmative action there would be significantly fewer black attorneys in the United States. David L. Chambers and Richard O. Lempert are professors of law at University of*

David L. Chambers, Timothy T. Clydesdale, William C. Kidder, and Richard O. Lempert, "The Real Impact of Eliminating Affirmative Action in American Law Schools: An Empirical Critique of Richard Sander's Study," *Stanford Law Review*, vol. 57, no. 6, May 2005, pp. 1855–98. Republished with permission of *Stanford Law Review*, conveyed through Copyright Clearance Center, Inc.

Michigan Law School. Timothy T. Clydesdale is a professor of sociology at the College of New Jersey and William C. Kidder is a researcher at the Equal Justice Society.

As you read, consider the following questions:

1. Why do the authors suggest using 2003 law school admissions data rather than 2001 data?

2. According to the authors, if affirmative action programs were ended, the numbers of new African American attorneys would decline by what percent each year?

3. According to the authors, some law schools would perceive a benefit if affirmative action programs were ended. Which law schools and why?

In his article, *A Systemic Analysis of Affirmative Action in American Law Schools,* Richard Sander reviews the history of affirmative action at American law schools and the litigation in the courts. He attacks the Supreme Court's handling of the evidence before it in *Grutter v. Bollinger,* claiming that the the University of Michigan Law School gave greater weight to race in admissions than the majority of the Court recognized. The bulk of Sander's article, however, is a speculative inquiry into what would happen to matriculation, graduation and bar passage by African American students at American law schools if race were no longer taken into account in admissions decisions. It is this central section of the Sander article to which this response is addressed.

## Rosy Forecasts Wrong

Sander makes an astonishing forecast: that there would be more black lawyers without affirmative action than there are with it. His counterintuitive prediction is based on the theory that if affirmative action in admissions were ended, some African American students who are admitted to a law school today would no longer be admitted at all, but that many more of the African Americans who would be admitted to law school by race-neutral criteria would graduate and pass the bar than is the case today. They would perform better, he argues, because, with the end of affirmative action, they would attend schools where their entering credentials are like those of their white classmates and where they would graduate and pass the bar at the same rate as whites. Spinning out a series of assumptions and projections, he concludes that, if affirmative action were ended, there would be an 8.8 percent net increase in the numbers of African American attorneys entering the bar each year. . . .

The four of us have drafted this response because we believe that Sander's forecasts are irresponsible. We believe that an even-handed assessment of available data on law school admissions, law school performance, and bar exam performance will show that Sander's article is premised upon a series of statistical errors, oversights, and implausible (and at times internally contradictory) assumptions. Sander blames affirmative action for a host of performance disparities between white and African American students that the data simply do not support. Our critique combines an independent analysis of Sander's data with other more recent sources that Sander neglected. Our own conclusion is that if affirmative action in admissions were eliminated, there would probably be a 25 to 30 percent decline in the numbers of African Americans entering the bar, not the rosy 8.8 percent improvement that he forecasts.

## Significant Mistakes

Sander makes insupportable (and invariably rosy) predictions about the effects of ending affirmative action on every stage that law students pass through on their way to becoming practitioners—in particular, on application levels, matriculation, graduation and passage of the bar. Here are his most significant mistakes:

## Admissions and Matriculation

Sander acknowledges that with an end of affirmative action many African Americans who matriculate at law school would no longer be admitted at all, but, drawing on a study of admissions data from 2001, calculates that the decline in admissions and matriculation would be only 14 percent. He is wrong. The actual reduction in the numbers of African Americans who would enter law school would be much greater because:

- 2001 was an abnormal admissions year, with an unusually low number of white applicants and a higher than usual ratio of black to white applicants; using admissions data from 2003, which is more typical of historical patterns, we conclude that the proportion of African American students who could no longer secure admission to any law school if affirmative action ended would be at least 24 percent, not the 14 percent that Sander believes.

- In addition, Sander assumes that, after affirmative action ends, every African American who could still get into some law school somewhere would actually apply to that law school and decide to matriculate there. Every single one. This is absurd. With an end of affirmative action, applications by promising African American candidates are almost certain to decline to some extent. Some, particularly those attending highly selective undergraduate institutions now, will abandon law and pick other career paths rather than attend a law school that seems to have little prestige or attend a law school where only one or two of their classmates are black. Some others, no longer able to get into a school nearby, will be unwilling to apply to regional law schools hundreds or thousands of miles away.

> ## Our Preliminary Estimates of the Effects of Eliminating Law School Affirmative Action on the Production of African American Attorneys
>
> (*Synthesizing Data from 1991 Matriculants and 2003-2004 Applicants*)
>
> | Stage of the system | Our estimate of change by eliminating affirmative action |
> | --- | --- |
> | Applicants | −10% to −15% |
> | Admittees | −35% to −45% |
> | Matriculants | −40% to −45% |
> | Graduates | −35% to −40% |
> | Passing the Bar | −25% to −30% |
>
> TAKEN FROM: "The Real Impact of Eliminating Affirmative Action in American Law Schools," *Stanford Law Review*, November 2004.

- When we couple the 24 percent of African American candidates who could no longer secure admission anywhere with the additional group that might be admitted but who would no longer apply to a school that would accept them, we believe that the decline in matriculations of African American students might well approach 40 to 45 percent.

## Grades in Law School and Rates of Graduation

Sander forecasts that if affirmative action ended, African American students would attend schools where their LSAT [Law School Admissions Test] scores and undergraduate grades would be the same as their white classmates and that they would then secure grades as high as their classmates and graduate at comparable rates. He believes they would do as well because in a study he conducted in the mid-nineties of first-semester, first-year grades, he found that once LSAT scores and UGPAs [Undergraduate Grade Point Average] were controlled for, black law students did as well as their white classmates. However, for two reasons, it remains likely that, even if schools rigorously applied race-neutral admissions criteria, African American students would still perform less well in law school and graduate at lower rates than their white classmates.

- First, at any given school that applies race-neutral criteria and admits all their students from a pool of applicants within the same above-average range of LSAT scores and undergraduate grades, it is still highly likely that within that pool, African American applicants will have somewhat lower LSATs and UGPAs than white applicants, simply because that is the way that white and African American students are distributed in the national pool. That is to say, at any given law school, African American applicants are more likely to be in the lower half of the school's applicant pool than they are to be in the upper half. Accordingly, the African American students admitted to most law schools are highly likely to have somewhat lower entry credentials than whites who are admitted even with a race-neutral selection system. If the LSATs and UGPAs of admitted African American students are lower, then by Sander's own reasoning, their grades in law school would likely remain lower and their rates of graduation lower as well.

- Second, despite Sander's claims, research by others strongly suggests that, in general, African American students do not in fact perform as well as whites within the same law schools even when they have similar LSATs and UGPAs. Something about the atmosphere of law school exacerbates the entering educational gaps of minority and other atypical law students. It is not African Americans alone who get lower grades than their entry numbers would predict. Latino students, Asian American students, and students who begin law school when they are 30 or older suffer a similar fate.

# Bar Passage

The most recent research on bar passage by race, conducted in the mid-1990s, found that a much higher proportion of African Americans than whites who took the bar exam one or more times never passed it. Sander believes that most of this gap in the pass rate between African Americans and whites is due to affirmative action: some African Americans fail the bar because they should never have been admitted to law school at all; others fail because they could properly be admitted to some school somewhere but have attended schools where they are over their heads and fail to learn enough to pass the bar. He believes that if they went to law schools where their entry credentials were the same as whites, they would do as well as whites. Again, his reasoning is flawed.

- In the preceding section, we pointed out the reasons why African Americans admitted to law schools under wholly race-neutral criteria are unlikely to perform as well in law school as their white classmates. Since Sander's expectation that African Americans will do as well as their white classmates on the bar is based entirely on his unjustified belief that they will do as well in law school grades, his conclusion that they will do as well on the bar is also flawed.

# Overall Reduction in the Number of African-American Attorneys

Putting together the effects at admission, graduation and bar passage of ending affirmative action, we believe that, while it is probably the case that if affirmative action were ended the graduation rate of African American students would improve somewhat at the law schools they would then attend, the net impact of ending affirmative action would be calamitous— probably in the range of a 25–30 percent decline overall in the numbers of new African American attorneys each year.

# Where African-American Law Students Would Go to Law School with an End to Affirmative Action

Ending affirmative action would not have the same effects across all law schools. Some law schools would perceive a benefit, particularly those in large urban areas that compete with nearby elite schools and currently have difficulty matriculating many African American students with reasonably high LSATs and UGPAs. These schools might end up with more African American students with promising admissions credentials. On the other hand, at a very large number of law schools, a massive reduction in the numbers of African American students would almost certainly occur.

Sander concedes that ending affirmative action would reduce the percentage of African American students at the "most elite" schools from their current level of around eight percent down to about one or two percent. He implies that the decrease would be very modest at schools other than the most elite. In this he surely errs again. Our analysis of the redistribution that ending affirmative action would cause is more preliminary than our analysis of total numbers above, but our estimates so far suggest that ending affirmative action and applying strictly race neutral criteria at admissions would lead to a severe decline in the number of African American students not just at the ten or twenty most selective law schools, but at least at the fifty or so most selective. We believe that the effect of cutting out about three-fourths of the African American students at the country's most highly regarded law schools would harm not only African Americans seeking to be lawyers but also white students and the nation as a whole.

We believe that performance disparities between African Americans and whites in law school and on bar exams raise serious and important issues that law schools and the profession must address, but we reject Sander's proposal to end affirmative action as a solution. Indeed, because Sander's conclusion—that "blacks as a whole would be unambiguously better off" without affirmative action—is based upon such a weak chain of untenable estimates and assumptions, we are concerned that if left unchallenged in the legal academy and elsewhere, Sander's article may improperly discourage many African Americans from applying to law school, thus irresponsibly contributing to the very problem Sander purports to remedy.

*"[D]espite the possibility that Asian Americans may be the group most 'disadvantaged' by affirmative action, they consistently, vigorously and over-whelmingly support it at the polls."*

# Asian Americans Support Affirmative Action

*Richard Kim*

*In this viewpoint, Richard Kim says even though Asian Americans as a group would benefit the most from the end of race-based preferences, most Asians want to keep affirmative action programs. Asians are already disproportionately represented at elite colleges, and their numbers would undoubtedly increase if affirmative action were to end; however, according to Kim, Asian Americans wholeheartedly support affirmative action, largely because they still remember the pain of past discrimination directed against them. Kim is a columnist for* The Nation *and teaches in the American Studies Department at Skidmore College.*

Richard Kim, "Asian Americans for Affirmative Action," *The Nation*, January 9, 2007. www.thenation.com. Copyright © 2007 by *The Nation* Magazine/The Nation Company, Inc. Reproduced by permission.

As you read, consider the following questions:

1. Since the passage of Proposition 209 in California, how much has the Asian student population grown at the University of California, Berkeley?
2. What did the study by Espenshade and Chung find?
3. Give two examples of legacy discrimination against Asians.

Sunday's [Jan. 7, 2007] *NYT* [*New York Times*] Education supplement ran a cover story by Timothy Egan about Asian Americans and affirmative action. Focusing on UC [University of California] Berkeley—where Asians have grown to 41% of the student body since Proposition 209 banned racial preferences in 1997—Egan observes that the end of affirmative action and the implementation of a "pure meritocracy" in admissions spells hugely disproportionate numbers of Asians at elite colleges and drastic shortages of Hispanics and African Americans. Berkeley, he concludes somewhat ominously, is the future of higher education.

## The Numbers

But you don't need the *NYT* to spot the trend. Just take a day trip to the Ivy league campus of your choice. Back when I was at Yale (in the mid-'90s), Kim was the most common last name. Outdoing the Jones by far, there were, I think, 51 of us at one point. (There were even, to my chagrin, two Richard Kims!) As Egan points out, Asian Americans comprise roughly 5% of the U.S. population but represent anywhere from 13–40% of undergraduates at many top schools: 27% at MIT [Massachusetts Institute of Technology], 24% at Stanford, 17% at UT [University of Texas] Austin, 13% at Columbia, 37% in the UC system as a whole and so forth. In contrast, only 3.6% of Berkeley's freshman class are African American and only 11% are Hispanic—way below state population levels.

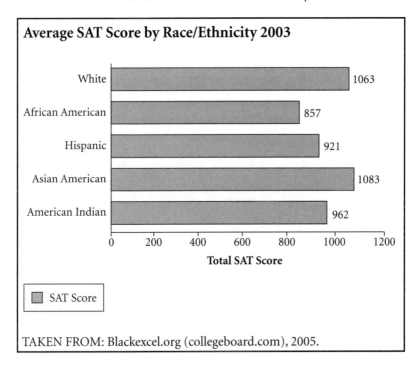

## Average SAT Score by Race/Ethnicity 2003

| Race/Ethnicity | SAT Score |
|---|---|
| White | 1063 |
| African American | 857 |
| Hispanic | 921 |
| Asian American | 1083 |
| American Indian | 962 |

Total SAT Score

■ SAT Score

TAKEN FROM: Blackexcel.org (collegeboard.com), 2005.

Egan's right about the numbers, but he misses the mark on many other measures. First, he underplays the differences between "brain drain" Asian Americans and more recent [as of 2007], less affluent, less educated Asian immigrants. As Frank Wu points out in his book *Yellow: Race in America Beyond Black and White*, after the passage of Prop. 209, Filipino Americans (like African Americans) were "zeroed out" at Berkeley's law school despite the fact that the Bay Area contains one of the largest Filipino communities in the US. Egan does quote a few academics who note that Sri Lankans and Koreans are not the same people, but he makes it seem as if the salient differences are matters of culture and "values" rather than of class and access.

## Asian Americans Back Affirmative Action

Secondly, for much of the article Egan gives the erroneous impression that Asian Americans are just delighted about their demographic surge at the UCs, biting to end affirmative action elsewhere and seize seats currently reserved for other minorities. He gives airtime to Jian Li, who's campaigning to deny Princeton federal funding because he thinks its admission policy discriminates against Asian Americans. (Despite a perfect SAT score, Li was rejected by the Tigers. But don't shed a tear just yet, he's doing quite fine at Yale.) And Egan cites a 2005 study by Thomas J. Espenshade and Chang Y. Chung that finds that, without affirmative action, Asians (and not whites) would fill the vast majority (80%) of spots reserved for African Americans and Hispanics at elite universities. But what Egan fails to note here is that, despite the possibility that Asian Americans may be the group most "disadvantaged" by affirmative action, they consistently, vigorously and overwhelmingly support it at the polls. Back in 1996, California governor Pete Wilson, Ward Connerly and a host of other right-wingers ran a vicious, race-wedge campaign for Prop. 209. Asian communities were targeted with a slew of invidious, "me-first" messages designed to appeal to their narrow self-interests. And yet, 61% of Asian American voters rejected Prop. 209. Last year [2006], when Michigan voters approved a similar measure (Prop. 2) by 58%, 75% of Asian American voters voted against it. Joining the NAACP [National Association for the Advancement of Colored People], Rainbow/Push Coalition, the ACLU [American Civil Liberties Union] and the UAW [United Auto Workers] in mobilizing opposition to Prop. 2 was the Asian American Legal Defense and Education Fund.

The real question then about Asian Americans and affirmative action—one that Egan and the *NYT* don't ask—is why? Why do we continue to support a policy that apparently "harms" us? One answer is that it doesn't, at least not always and not equally. Connerly and his minions—who have anti-affirmative action initiatives brewing in Arizona, Colorado, Missouri and Nebraska—have focused their message almost exclusively on admissions, and not on public employment and state contracts, even though affirmative action applies to those arenas as well, arenas in which Asian Americans are often underrepresented. (By focusing solely on Prop. 209's impact on UC admissions, the *NYT* repeats Connerly's misinformation.)

But racial group interest aside, I have a hunch that Asian Americans support affirmative action because the legacy of discrimination against Asians—from the Chinese Exclusion Act of 1882 to Japanese internment to the crucifixion of Wen Ho Lee to post-9/11 roundups of brown folk—is seared into our collective memory. And despite the model minority myth, and despite the occasional con-jobs like Dinesh d'Souza or Elaine Chao, most of us know that the deck isn't fairly stacked, that the moment demands remedy, for us and for others.

## The End of the White Republic?

The last question I'll raise is: What's up with white people? If abolishing affirmative action would gain whites little in the admissions game (and then mostly to the ruling class of whites) and if Asian Americans reap most of the benefits of what Egan calls a "pure meritocracy," then why is it that only white people as a group vote to end affirmative action? Why are the litigants and campaigners at the forefront of the affirmative action backlash predominately white (Connerly aside)? From where does this seething, misplaced, amnesiac resentment, so often masquerading as class-consciousness (see Walter Benn Michaels) and fairness, come?

Egan's article, if unwittingly, at least provides a clue. In his Bladerunner-esque, dystopian image of Berkeley as "Asian heaven," as "boring socially, full of science nerds, a hard place to make friends," as abuzz with "foreign languages" and packed with "clubs representing every conceivable ethnic group," lies the real anxiety behind the white backlash—the unnerving, inevitable end of the white republic. If Berkeley is indeed the future of America, then neither maintaining nor abolishing af-

> *"Because of the superior performance of Asian students on high school grades and pre-college aptitude tests, many colleges and universities, through unannounced policies, place these 'minority students' at the back of the line."*

# Affirmative-Action Programs Discriminate Against Asians

*Larry Elder*

*In this viewpoint, Larry Elder poses the question, what would the reaction be if the National Basketball Association (NBA) tried to implement affirmative action to make the league more diverse? The outcry would be deafening, says Elder. But, he explains, this is what is happening to Asian American students at many of the nation's elite colleges and universities. Elder says that colleges turn away many exceedingly qualified Asian Americans in order to make room for less qualified blacks and Hispanics. Elder is an author and the host of a nationally syndicated radio show.*

As you read, consider the following questions:

    1. When did California outlaw race-based preferences?

2. Compare the SAT median score for Asians entering the University of Michigan to the median score for whites and blacks.

3. What are some reasons Elder suggests to explain why Asians have not filed more lawsuits?

I magine the following press release:

> In a closed-door meeting, the owners voted to limit the number of black players, in order to increase attendance from non-black customers. The NBA now consists of over 80 percent black players, which creates a non-diverse and less enlightening experience for the predominately non-black fan. Thus, in order to continue basketball's popularity, the NBA determines player diversity a necessity to maintain the game's prosperity. —NBA commissioner David Stern.

Before you could say "Michael Richards," in swoop the Revs. Jesse Jackson and Al Sharpton, as well as the other usual suspect "black leaders." Marching, screaming, stomping and howling will precede enough lawsuits to keep the entire American and National Bar Associations fully employed for the next decade.

## Affirmative Action Hurts Asian-American Students

Yet when it comes to colleges and universities admitting Asian-American students, this is, in effect, exactly what is happening. Because of the superior performance of Asian students on high school grades and pre-college aptitude tests, many colleges and universities, through unannounced policies, place these "minority students" at the back of the line.

California, in 1996, outlawed race-based preferences. After this new law, the percentage of Asian students enrolled at the elite, competitive campus of UC [University of California] Berkeley increased from 34.6 percent to 42 percent by fall

## Diversity Isn't Good for Asians

It's time to admit that "diversity" is code for racism. If it makes you feel better, we can call it "nice" racism or "well-intentioned" racism or "racism that's good for you." Except that's the rub: It's racism that may be good for you if "you" are a diversity guru, a rich white liberal, a college administrator or one of sundry other types. But the question of whether diversity is good for "them" is a different question altogether, and much more difficult to answer.

If by "them" you mean minorities such as Jews, Chinese-Americans, Indian-Americans and other people of Asian descent, then the ongoing national obsession with diversity probably isn't good.

Jewish World Review, *November 15, 2006.*

2006. Similarly, the state of Washington outlawed preferences in 1998, and Asian enrollment at the University of Washington increased from 22.1 percent to 25.4 percent by 2004. Michigan recently passed laws outlawing the use of race in government hiring, contracting and admission into public colleges and universities. Expect an increase in the Asian student body at the University of Michigan.

Question: Why do Asian students and their parents put up with it?

## Jian Li Complaint

Jian Li does not intend to. Li, a permanent U.S. resident, immigrated to America from China at the age of 4. He graduated at the top 1 percent of his high school class. On his SATs, he received a perfect 2400, and totaled 2390 (10 points less than perfection) on his SAT II subject tests in math and science. Yet Li received rejections from Princeton, Harvard, Stanford, the University of Pennsylvania and MIT [Massachusetts Institute of Technology] Li is not alone. Attorney Don Joe from Asian-American Politics, an enrollment-tracking Internet site—says he receives complaints "from Asian-American parents about how their children have excellent grades and scores but are being rejected by the most selective colleges. It appears to be an open secret."

Li filed a complaint with the Department of Education's Office for Civil Rights, with the matter currently under review. On his college applications, Li left blank his country of origin and his race, although he did put down his citizenship and listed Chinese as his first language spoken and the language spoken at home. Inquires about his race, said Li, "[S]eemed very irrelevant to me, if not offensive."

Why did he sue? Li said he wants to "send a message to the admissions committee to be more cognizant of possible bias, and that the way they're conducting admissions is not equitable."

## Asian Students Take a Hit

A study of the University of Michigan's 2005 applicants by the Center for Equal Opportunity documented the hit that white and Asian students take because of race-based preferences. In an apparent desire to increase the number of blacks and Hispanics, the school admitted Asian applicants with a median SAT score of 1400 (out of a possible 1600 for the test in use at that time). This made the Asian median 50 points higher than the median for admitted white students; 140 points higher than Hispanics; and 240 points higher than blacks. Of Asian students with 1240 on the SAT and a high school GPA of 3.2 in 2005, only 10 percent got into Michigan. But 14 percent of whites with those stats were admitted, as were 88 percent of Hispanics and 92 percent of blacks.

What's more, the "boost" given to Hispanic and Latino students by racial preferences often backfires. Peter Kirsanow, a member of the U.S. Commission on Civil Rights and a black attorney, said, "Would college administrators continue to mouth platitudes about affirmative action if their students knew that preferential admissions cause black law students to flunk out at two-and-a-half times the rate of whites? Or that black law students are six times less likely to pass the bar? Or that half of black law students never become lawyers?"

What took Asians so long to figure this out and file more lawsuits?

Perhaps Asians remain unaware of the damage these policies do to their own admission possibilities. Perhaps they consider themselves a discriminated minority, and thus support programs to "offset" the negative effects of their perceived opposition. Or perhaps they feel that despite the negative effect of race-based preferences on their own possibilities of admission, they feel sympathetic toward to the "need" to "help" blacks and Hispanics. Who knows?

In any case, 17-year-old freshman Jian Li now attends Yale. Not a bad foundation for a future. Just ask Yale law school grad and former President Bill Clinton, who, by the way, supports race-based preferences.

# Periodical Bibliography

*The following articles have been selected to supplement the diverse views presented in this chapter.*

Linda Chavez      "Ending Racial Preferences: It's About Time," *Townhall.com*, April 27, 2007.

Ellis Cose      "The Color of Change; Why Are We Still Debating Whether Race Should Be a Factor in College Admissions?" *Newsweek*, November 13, 2006.

Lisa Takeuchi Cullen      "The Diversity Delusion," *Time*, May 7, 2007.

Euel W. Elliott and Andrew I. E. Ewoh      "Beyond Gratz and Grutter: Prospects for Affirmative Action in the Aftermath of the Supreme Court's Michigan Decisions," *Review of Policy Research*, July 2005.

Eryn Hadley      "Did the Sky Really Fall? Ten Years After California's Proposition 209," Program for Judicial Awareness Working Paper, no. 05-006, August 11, 2005.

Jack Hitt      "Mighty White of You: Racial Preferences Color America's Oldest Skulls and Bones," *Harper's Magazine*, July 2005.

Ira Katznelson      "New Deal, Raw Deal: How Aid Became Affirmative Action for Whites," *Washington Post*, September 27, 2005.

Jay Mathews      "Should Colleges Have Quotas for Asian Americans?" *Washington Post*, October 12, 2004.

David Luc Nguyen      "Taking Affirmative Action: Do Gays Deserve the Same Boost into College as Racial Minorities?" *Advocate*, January 30, 2007.

Christopher Shea      "Victim of Success? Are Asian-American Students Discriminated Against in College Admissions?" *Boston Globe*, November 26, 2006.

# Chapter 4

# What Impact Does the Government Have on Discrimination in the U.S.?

# Chapter Preface

Throughout its history, the U.S. government has struggled with discrimination. At times, such as when slavery was allowed or when states enacted "Black Codes," the government was a party to discrimination. These injustices were generally followed by government laws and policies that outlawed discrimination and sought to protect the civil rights of all Americans. Most civil rights statutes and constitutional amendments were enacted during two periods in U.S. history: from 1865 to 1877, or Reconstruction, and from 1957 to 1969, the era of the civil rights movement. During Reconstruction the U.S. government adopted several important legal measures protecting civil rights and outlawing discrimination.

Three Constitutional amendments were adopted during Reconstruction, starting with the Thirteenth Amendment in 1865. This amendment abolished slavery in the United States. It declares, "*Neither slavery nor involuntary servitude, except as a punishment for crime whereof the party shall have been duly convicted, shall exist within the United States, or any place subject to their jurisdiction.*" The amendment was ratified— adopted by three-fourths, or twenty-seven of the then thirty-six states in existence—on December 6, 1865. Eventually all thirty-six states would ratify the amendment, most in 1866. Mississippi, however, waited over one hundred years, ratifying the Thirteenth Amendment in 1995.

The Fourteenth Amendment was proposed in 1866 and ratified in 1868. It overturned the "Black Codes" which had been enacted by various states after the end of slavery. These codes severely restricted the newfound freedoms of former slaves. Blacks were compelled to work or risk being arrested. They were prevented from raising their own crops, marrying someone from a different race, and even from "roaming." Blacks had to obtain permission to enter many towns. The

Fourteenth Amendment ensures that no state "shall make or enforce any law which shall abridge the privileges or immunities of the citizens of the United States . . . [or] deprive any person of life, liberty, or property without due process of law, [or] deny to any person within its jurisdiction the equal protection of the laws." The Fifteenth Amendment was passed in 1870. It decreed that the right to vote could not be denied because of race, color, or previous condition of servitude. This finally gave non-white men the right to vote in the United States.

Several civil rights statutes were also enacted during Reconstruction. The Civil Rights Act of 1866 was enacted despite being vetoed by President Andrew Johnson. It overturned the U.S. Supreme Court's decision in the *Dred Scot* case, which had held that blacks were not and never could be U.S. citizens. This declared that all freed slaves were citizens and that anyone born on U.S. soil was a U.S. citizen, excluding Native Americans—they would not be officially granted citizenship until the enactment of the Indian Citizenship Act of 1924. The act also prohibited employment discrimination based on race and color and made it illegal to discriminate in housing based on race. The 1871 Civil Rights Act was enacted to protect southern blacks from the violence of the Ku Klux Klan (KKK), a white supremacist group. The act helped to destroy the first incarnation of the KKK, thus the 1871 Civil Rights Act is also known as the Ku Klux Klan (KKK) Act.

In 1875, the Congress passed the last Reconstruction-era civil rights statute. The Civil Rights Act of 1875 guaranteed blacks the same treatment as whites in certain public places. It was passed in response to the actions of many white business owners who refused to serve blacks in inns, railroads, and other public places. The Civil Rights Act of 1875 prohibited racial discrimination in such places and guaranteed "full and equal enjoyment" of such places. After passage of this act, eighty-two years went by before another civil rights statute was passed.

> *"The legal rules aren't perfect or infallible—because the accuser has to prove discrimination . . . but they do offer a systematic way of thinking through claims of bias and of determining when it's reasonable to infer bigotry from circumstances."*

# Anti-Discrimination Laws Aren't Perfect, but They Work

**Richard Thompson Ford**

*In the following viewpoint, Richard Thompson Ford uses an example from baseball to show that even when racist motives are obscured, anti-discrimination laws are effective in determining when legitimate discrimination has occurred. Ford uses the home run record first established by white baseball player Babe Ruth in the 1930s and eventually broken by black baseball player Hank Aaron in 1974. In the summer of 2006, controversial baseball player Barry Bonds, who is black, became only the second man (after Aaron) to have a chance to pass Ruth's homerun mark. Murmurs of racism were heard as many people openly displayed their unhappiness about this fact. Using Bonds as an* example, Ford describes how anti-discrimination law teases out legitimate discrimination from the circumstances. Bonds broke Ruth's record on May 28, 2006. Through 2006 he had hit a total of 734 home runs. When Ford wrote this piece, Aaron's record of 755 home runs still stood. Bonds hit his 756th home run on August 7, 2007. Ford is an author and professor of law at Stanford Law School.

As you read, consider the following questions:

1. How do the rules of the game (i.e. anti-discrimination law) establish discrimination?
2. What are mixed-motive anti-discrimination cases?
3. Why does Ford consider mixed-motives cases to be tough?

B arry Bonds officially "broke" Babe Ruth's home run record over Memorial Day weekend [May 28, 2006]. I put "broke" in scare quotes because, of course, that record hadn't been in one piece since 1974, when Hank Aaron broke it. Some baseball fans didn't want Aaron to break the Bambino's record—he received threats and hate mail from bigots who wanted to send black players back to the separate and unequal Negro Leagues.

More than 30 years later, with Bonds nearing Babe Ruth's career record, as many fans jeered as cheered. Bonds reports receiving threats and hate mail on a regular basis. And the press has not exactly written love letters. Is Bonds as much a victim of racism today as Aaron was in 1974? Anti-discrimination law offers a way to think about the question.

## Bonds, Aaron, and Ruth

Bonds himself thinks fans have it in for him for racial reasons "because Babe Ruth is one of the greatest baseball players ever and Babe Ruth ain't black. I'm black. Blacks, we go through a little more, and that's the truth." Others agree. Torii Hunter of the Minnesota Twins insisted in a *USA Today* interview, "It's so obvious what's going on. . . . It's killing me because you know it's about race." Danny Glover similarly mused on ESPN's *Bonds on Bonds* program: "I'm surprised the black community hasn't come out and made a statement about this." And Louisiana State University Professor Leonard Moore insists things are actually *worse* than when Hank Aaron was at bat: "White America doesn't want him to [pass] Babe Ruth and is doing everything they can to stop him. . . . I think what he'll go through will be 100 times worse than what Aaron went through."

There's one problem with this Bonds/Aaron comparison: No one thought Aaron had cheated. Bonds, on the other hand, is widely believed to have used performance-enhancing steroids—a belief backed up by evidence as unambiguous as a pair of 16-inch biceps, leaked testimony from a federal grand jury, and documents seized from the founder of the Bay Area Laboratory Co-operative [BALCO], where the steroids were made, and from Bonds' former trainer. And while fans and the press might give a smooth-talking charmer the benefit of any doubt, Bonds isn't exactly Mr. Congeniality: He's notorious for snubbing fans and teammates alike, fuming and brooding in the dugout, and refusing to sign autographs.

## Smoking out the Real Motives

So, maybe jeering fans are really angry not because a black man surpassed Babe Ruth's record but because a surly, arrogant jerk used steroids to pass Babe Ruth's record. Most of the people who have weighed in on the controversy assume it has to be either one or the other. But maybe it's some of both. Is there a way to tease out the real motives here?

This is a complicated inquiry, in part because there are no fans shouting racial epithets, wearing white hoods, or burning crosses at Giants games. Instead, they're shouting "cheater" and holding up signs about BALCO. Modern racism, unlike the blatant racism of the Jim Crow era, is usually covert. Few people will admit to racist motivations—even to themselves. So, we have fewer and fewer cases where the evidence of racism is unambiguous, and more and more where we have to smoke out concealed discriminatory motives. Is it fair to surmise that many fans who claim to be put off by steroids are really put off by skin color?

Civil rights law has developed a way to deal with these subtler cases. Some involve an either-or question. Suppose a black employee is overlooked for a promotion. Either the employee was not promoted because of race or she was not promoted for a legitimate reason. The employee bats first: She has to show it's plausible that she was the victim of discrimination. She can do this by eliminating the most obvious good reasons she might have been passed over—she wasn't qualified, or the position she wanted was eliminated or had already been filled. If she does this she's on base, but it's not a run yet. The employer now has a chance to respond that he was motivated by a legitimate reason—say, the employee's bad attitude or alleged steroid use.

## Single Motive

At this point the employee can still score if she shows that the legitimate reason offered by the employer is a "pretext," and that the real motivation is race. The rules of the game thus let us establish discriminatory motives by process of elimination: If we eliminate all of the legitimate reasons, we can deduce that the reason must be unlawful bias. We call these "single motive" cases because the proof structure is based on the presumption that there's only one true motive: Either it's a good one or a discriminatory one.

Bonds doesn't have much of a single-motive case. His notorious surliness, combined with the steroid scandal, are good, nondiscriminatory reasons for fans to hiss and jeer rather than clap and cheer. Of course Bonds might argue that ste-

## Ruth's Record Not Pure

Ruth's 714 home run record lacks the spit-shined purity his backers trumpet. The Sultan of Swat made his bones playing against only a select segment of the population because of the ban on players whose skin color ran brown to black. Ruth never had to hit against Negro League greats Satchel Paige or Lefty Mathis to amass the magic 714. Yet no asterisk for institutionalized racism mars the Babe's marks. Ruth also was a habitual user of a banned substance that was deemed unambiguously illegal by the federal government—a drug Ruth believed enhanced his performance: alcohol. Ruth was a star during the roaring prohibition 1920s, and as teammate Joe Dugan said, "Babe would go day and night, broads and booze."

*Dave Zirin, "Bonding with the Babe,"*
The Nation, *May 8, 2006. www.thenation.com.*

roids and personality are mere pretexts—the real reason fans and the press don't like him is race. But no doubt a lot of people are sincerely upset about the steroid scandal. When someone cheats, fans are justified in feeling, well, cheated. The "pretext" pitch is outside the strike zone.

## Mixed Motives

But what if fans dislike Bonds because of his personality, or the steroid scandal *and* his race? Maybe they'd be willing to overlook the same flaws in a white player. In the law we'd call this a claim of "mixed motives." Here, a legitimate reason for the decision isn't enough to end the game; the employer still can be held liable for discrimination if bigotry was also in play.

*Price Waterhouse v. Hopkins*, the case that established mixed-motives analysis, involved a woman who had been passed over for partnership at a large accounting firm. She had done good work for the firm and had hit a home run by landing a large contract the year she was up for promotion. But she had a bad personality: She was rude to coworkers, abrasive, difficult—sound like any major league sluggers you know? The firm said she was passed over because of her poor interpersonal skills. She said the reason was her sex: There were very few female partners at the firm, and some partners had made sexist comments about her, including calling her "macho" and telling her to wear makeup and jewelry and go to charm school. So, was she passed over because of her sex or because of her abrasive personality?

The Supreme Court disagreed about how to sort this out: In fact, the Court split four ways, with four justices in a plurality, three in dissent, and each of the remaining two writing separate concurrences. The upshot of the plurality opinion, however, was that if the employee can show that bigotry played a role in the decision, she *might* have a case. At that point, the employer can get off the hook only by showing it would have made the same decision even if bigotry hadn't been in the mix. Mixed-motives cases are tough because they often involve unsympathetic victims and ambiguous facts. It's hard to feel moral outrage on behalf of a wrongdoer or a troublemaker, even when they might also be victims of bigotry. And it's easy for bias to hide out in a crowd of good reasons that might justify the outcome. Making the right call in a mixed-motives case requires resolving conceptual puzzles and parsing obscure hypotheticals: Did the good reasons alone "justify" the decision? Would the decision have been the same even if no bigotry had been involved?

Would the press have hounded and fans booed a surly *white* steroid user closing in on Babe Ruth's career record? Obviously, there are no simple answers to such questions. So it's no surprise that the question of anti-Bonds sentiment is as controversial as the infield fly rule.

## Not Always Easy Answers

As the split on the Supreme Court suggests, even the most experienced umpires can't agree on how to resolve such issues. The split also suggests that the differing answers involved the justices' personal ideological divisions as much as factual ambiguities. Just as sports fans reflexively back their favorite team on close calls, when the facts surrounding a claim of racism are inscrutable or ambiguous, people tend to fall back on ideological predispositions. Saying Bonds is a victim of racism becomes a way of saying racism is still a serious problem in our society. Saying he's just bellyaching becomes a way of saying too many black people are playing the race card.

Team spirit is good sport at the ballpark after a few beers, but it's foul play when it comes to race relations. So, I'll to try to resist my home-team liberal reflexes and call the Bonds controversy as I see it: I think racism remains a serious social problem, but I don't see much evidence of it here. When a black person is treated badly *for no good reason*, it's reasonable to suspect the reason was race. But this inference can't be justified when there is a good reason; then we need some other evidence that bias was a significant factor—like the evidence that partners at Price Waterhouse said Ann Hopkins was too "macho" and needed to be more feminine. And we don't have that kind of evidence here.

Bonds is right to say that blacks "go through a little more" because some people are racists: Hank Aaron was deluged with explicitly racist hate mail and death threats and needed police protection in the dugout as he closed in on Babe Ruth's record. No doubt some of those bigots are still out there, and unfortunately, new ones have been spawned since. Things have improved since the 1970s, but we haven't beaten racism yet. However, this *general* observation can't be enough to support a *specific* claim of bias in this case, just as workplace sexism generally wouldn't have been enough to support Ann Hopkins' claim that Price Waterhouse discriminated against *her.* Without more to back it up, the claim that Bonds is a victim of racism is just speculation. We can't assume that anytime a black person is treated badly we can or should blame racism—especially when he's done something to provoke the abuse.

The legal rules aren't perfect or infallible—because the accuser has to *prove* discrimination, they almost certainly miss some cases of bias where there's just not enough evidence—but they do offer a systematic way of thinking through claims of bias and of determining when it's reasonable to infer bigotry from circumstances. And in an environment where most claims of racial bias require close calls, that's as near as we're likely to get to a replay on Diamond Vision.

"This case suggests the limits of anti-discrimination law, which does seem fairly useless if its scope cannot comprehend the injustice apparent in this situation."

# Anti-Discrimination Laws Are Limited

*Stephanie M. Wildman*

*In the following viewpoint, Stephanie Wildman describes an incident that occurred at a Conoco gas station in Texas, where a Hispanic woman and her father were treated extremely poorly, assailed with racial slurs, and subsequently left the store without completing all of their purchases. The family claimed they had been racially discriminated against and sued Conoco under U.S. anti-discrimination law. However, the district court ruled against the family and in favor of Conoco, saying that discrimination was not proven. Wildman uses the incident to illustrate the limits of anti-discrimination law. Wildman is a professor of law and the director of the Center for Social Justice and Public Service at Santa Clara University School of Law.*

Stephanie M. Wildman, "The Persistence of White Privilege," *Santa Clara University Legal Studies Research Paper Series*, no. 06–07, August 2006, pp. 259–263. http://ssrn.com. Reproduced by permission of the author.

As you read, consider the following questions:

1. What three things did the family (the plaintiff) need to establish in order to prove they had been discriminated against?

2. Explain the significance to the final verdict of the fact that Govea voluntarily left his beer on the counter and that Arguello successfully completed her transaction.

3. According to Wildman, the lack of outrage at the result of the case illustrates what?

The absence of a privilege analysis in law can result in the perpetuation of injustice, as occurred in the case based on the following facts. In March 1995, Denise Arguello and her family, including her father Alberto Govea, stopped to purchase gas at a Conoco gas station in Fort Worth, Texas. After her husband pumped the gas, Ms. Arguello and her father entered the station's convenience store to pay for the gas and to purchase beer. They waited in line while Cindy Smith, a clerk, helped other customers. Fifth Circuit Judge Jerry E. Smith summarizes the testimony about what happened next:

## The Incident

Arguello testified that Smith was rude to her when she reached the counter and that her demeanor was less friendly than it had been with the customers she had previously served. After Arguello presented her credit card as payment, Smith requested identification. Arguello testified that Smith singled her out by demanding that she provide identification; Smith contends that she requested identification because Arguello was attempting to buy beer.

Arguello, an Oklahoma resident, presented Smith with her valid Oklahoma driver's license. Smith initially refused to accept it, claiming she could not take an out-of-state license, but she eventually accepted it and completed the transaction. During Arguello's purchase, Govea became increasingly frustrated with the manner in which Smith was treating his daughter. Consequently, he left the beer he had intended to purchase on the counter and walked out of the store.

After Smith completed Arguello's sale, the tension between them escalated into a confrontation. Arguello testified that Smith began shouting obscenities at her and making racially derogatory remarks. [According to the trial court memorandum opinion Arguello alleged that "Smith referred to her as a 'f—ing [sic] Iranian Mexican bitch.'" Arguello began to leave with her purchase, but realized that she had the wrong copy of the credit card slip and approached the counter again. After another argument, Arguello and Smith exchanged copies. As Arguello walked away the second time, Smith shoved a six-pack of beer off the counter and onto the floor.

Plaintiffs testified that after Arguello left the store, Smith began screaming racist remarks over the intercom. At the same time, Smith laughed at Arguello and her family and made several crude gestures. Govea and other family members telephoned Conoco from a payphone outside the store to lodge a complaint. During that telephone conversation, the Conoco official indicated that he wanted to know the name of the clerk in question. When Govea attempted to re-enter the store to determine Smith's name, Smith locked him out while laughing and making crude gestures.

## The Lawsuit

Arguello and Govea sued claiming race discrimination under 42 U.S.C. § 1981. A jury decided the case in their favor, but the district court granted Conoco's motion for a judgment as a matter of law. The Fifth Circuit affirmed the district court ruling in favor of Conoco.

The Fifth Circuit began its decision by reviewing the elements of a § 1981 claim:

## Stories of Discrimination

Their stories sound like tales from the pre-civil rights era. Terri Wise, 34, of Charlotte, browsed in a local Cracker Barrel store in 2001. Wise, who is African-American, says a white saleswoman followed her.

When she picked up a doll, as shoppers do, the saleswoman took it from her and put it back on the shelf. The same thing happened with a greeting card. When Wise looked around, she noticed a white patron touching merchandise freely—without supervision.

The Rev. Henry Harris, 55, also African-American, says that at a Cracker Barrel restaurant in Arkansas two years ago, he and his family watched for 35 minutes as white diners in parties of the same size who arrived after him were escorted to tables. He wound up in the smoking section "with other African-American patrons," even though he had requested non-smoking and tables were open there. When he appealed to a manager, he "politely looked at me and said if we were dissatisfied . . . there was a Burger King" around the corner.

*Julie Schmit and Larry Copeland,*
*"Cracker Barrel Customer Says Bias Was 'Flagrant,'"*
USA Today, *May 7, 2004. www.usatoday.com.*

[A] plaintiff must establish "(1) that she is a member of a racial minority; (2) that [the defendant] had intent to discriminate on the basis of race; and (3) that the discrimination concerned one or more of the activities enumerated in the statute."

The court acknowledged no dispute existed over plaintiffs' status as racial minorities and that the evidence had been sufficient to create a jury question as to whether they had suffered discrimination during their visit to defendant's store.

The court stated: "this case turns on the third element, namely, whether Smith's conduct implicated rights guaranteed by § 1981."

## The Verdict

Fifth Circuit law for establishing a denial of § 1981 rights in the retail setting requires evidence of an attempt to contract that was thwarted by the defendant merchant. The purchase must be thwarted, not merely deterred by the merchant. The Fifth Circuit stated that because Govea voluntarily left the beer on the counter and exited the store without trying to buy it, the clerk Smith did not prevent Govea from making the purchase. The court similarly found Arguello without remedy because she did "successfully complete the transaction."

Plaintiffs had argued for a broader interpretation of the statute that included "the making, performance, modification, and termination of contracts, and the enjoyment of all benefits, privileges, terms, and conditions of the contractual relationship." The court declined to follow this proposed broader application. Rather, it distinguished case law involving both discriminatory service in restaurants and clubs and other cases concerning discriminatory prepayment or check-writing policies.

## White Privilege Enabled Wrong Result

The lack of outrage surrounding the result illustrates another way that privilege operates. The decision does not merely reflect the view of an aberrational circuit court ignored by the Supreme Court in its denial of certiorari; the case also becomes precedent, setting the terms for appropriate future behavior. How will the general counsel of Conoco advise employees to act in the future? What advice might corporate counsel have given to employees if the result had come out differently? This decision permits subordination and abuse to continue without redress or even acknowledgment that it was wrong. That continuation reinscribes the white privilege that made the conduct and ensuing judicial decision possible. White privilege enabled the judges to cast Mr. Govea's transaction as a voluntary withdrawal from purchasing beer. Most likely, the judges had been to convenience stores much like this one, but they probably had not been welcomed with racial epithets. Life lived in the white comfort zone made it easy for judges to miss the injustice. The judges likely experienced their own convenience store visits as individuals. As individuals they were unable to see the group identification that represents the lived reality for non-whites. That reality means not only facing this kind of harassment but also never knowing when it will strike as one goes about the business of life. That fear of a world gone awry, like a rug pulled from under one's feet, has not been part of the white comfort zone. The push to colorblindness further supports law operating within these cultural practices to ignore the racialized reality in which the transaction took place. The judicial form of "taking back the center" maintains the status quo that led to the injustice.

## Limits of Law

Until law and the legal system address scenarios like that faced by Ms. Arguello and Mr. Govea, subordinating practices will continue. This case suggests the limits of antidiscrimination law, which does seem fairly useless if its scope cannot comprehend the injustice apparent in this situation. Reflecting on the inexplicable unfairness of key judicial decisions, Jerome Culp asked:

> How do you defend the tests in *Washington v. Davis*, the decision in *Bowers*, or the rule in *Korematsu*, the failure to apply prior principles in *McCleskey*, or the reasoning in *Shaw v. Reno?*

He answers his question, "The court ultimately simply responds that we the white majority have the power to do what we want in these cases." He reminds us that white judges, who do not face the same risk in making contracts as the Arguello family, have the power, reinforced by white privilege, to ignore the non-privileged reality. This failure to recognize privilege results in injustice like the *Arguello* case.

*"[T]he Constitution is color-blind. It is color-blind because the rule of law is color-blind, and because the idea of man himself—as reflected in the principles of the Declaration [of Independence]—is color-blind."*

# It Is Discriminatory for the Government to Consider Race

## Edward J. Erler

*In the following viewpoint, Edward J. Erler examines the meaning of "equal protection under the law" as prescribed in the Fourteenth Amendment to the U.S. Constitution. He contends that the Constitution, as it is written, is color-blind; therefore, the government should not consider race in any of its programs. This position suggests that programs that treat racial groups differently, such as affirmative action and racial preference, are unconstitutional. Erler also discusses the U.S. Civil Rights Act and the Gratz and Grutter Supreme Court cases challenging the University of Michigan's admissions policy. Erler has written extensively about the Constitutional government. He is a professor of political science at the California State University, San Bernardino.*

Edward J. Erler, "Is the Constitution Color-Blind?" *USA Today Magazine*, July 2004, pp. 60, 62–63. Copyright © 2004 Society for the Advancement of Education. Reproduced by permission.

As you read, consider the following questions:

1. The formal completion of the Constitution was achieved with the passage of what three amendments?
2. According to Erler, the Civil Rights Act of 1964 was a good expression of what?
3. What is the difference between a critical mass and a racial quota?

The 14th Amendment cannot be understood properly except in terms of the principles of the Declaration of Independence. The Constitution itself was written to denote those principles. Yet, insofar as it allowed slavery to continue, the Constitution is an incomplete expression. Slavery was a manifest violation of the central tenet of the Declaration that "all men are created equal," and of the injunction that just rule must therefore proceed from the consent of the governed. The Founding Fathers went as far as they could in this direction, given the political circumstances of the time. They could not go all the way, though. Understanding this, the drafters described the 14th Amendment as a completion of the Constitution. For instance, Thaddeus Stevens, a prominent member of the Joint Committee on Reconstruction, remarked that the framers were compelled by political necessity to postpone the "full establishment" of the principles of the Declaration "till a more propitious time. That time ought to be present now."

The formal completion of the Constitution actually was achieved with the passage of three amendments following the Civil War: the 13th, which abolished slavery; the 14th, which extended citizenship and civil rights to the newly freed slaves; and the 15th, which protected the right to vote against racial discrimination. However, this had to be translated into constitutional practice, a task that, in some sense, was the most difficult of all.

## The 14th Amendment: Equal Protection

The 14th Amendment, ratified in 1868, is the most important of the post-Civil War amendments. It established the first definition of citizenship in the Constitution, making Federal citizenship primary and state citizenship derivative, thereby securing the citizenship of newly freed slaves and nullifying the Supreme Court's 1857 *Dred Scott* decision that they were property. It also prohibited any state from abridging "the privileges or immunities" of Federal citizenship; from depriving "any person of life, liberty, or property without due process of law"; and from denying "to any person within its jurisdiction the equal protection of the laws." Each of these clauses has been, at one time or another, the center of fierce constitutional controversy. In the context of recent [as of 2004] affirmative action cases, the equal protection clause is most relevant.

Equal protection means first and foremost that every individual is guaranteed the equal protection of equal rights. These rights belong to individuals because they are inherent in human nature. In this sense, "all men are created equal" and no person has a right to rule another without his consent. Rights—both natural and civil—belong to individuals, not groups, and any attempt to condition the possession and enjoyment of rights on race or other class characteristics is a violation of equal protection. Race is an accidental, not an essential, feature of human nature, and the rule of law prohibits arbitrariness in its classification. Since race is an arbitrary category, it is excluded *ipso facto* by the rule of law. This is the principle behind Justice John Harlan's famous dissent in the 1896 case of *Plessy v. Ferguson*. The majority in that case—which concerned segregated railway cars—held that the law could treat people separately according to their race, as long as it treated them equally. Harlan disagreed, arguing that the Constitution is "color-blind." It is color-blind because the rule of law is color-blind, and because the idea of man himself—as reflected in the principles of the Declaration—is color-blind.

# The Civil Rights Act: Equal Protection of the Laws

The Civil Rights Act of 1964, in the tradition of Harlan's dissent, was a good expression of what the 14th Amendment meant by "equal protection of the laws." It prohibited discrimination against individuals on the basis of race, ethnicity, and religion. It embodied equal opportunity as its principle of distributive justice—the equal protection of equal rights. It required that natural talents and abilities, not artificial distinctions based on race or ethnicity, should be the measure of success. It insisted that rights belong to individuals, not racial classes or ethnic groups. The rule of law as the rule of reason—demanded no less. However, these noble aspirations of the Civil Rights Act almost immediately were deemed inadequate. In June 1965, Pres. Lyndon Johnson set the tone for a new vision of civil rights. "Freedom is not enough," he proclaimed. "It is not enough just to open the gates of opportunity. . . . We seek . . . not just equality as a right and a theory but equality as a fact and equality as a result. . . . To this end equal opportunity is essential, but not enough."

# Racial Preferences

The sweep of this pronouncement was breathtaking. If equal opportunity is not sufficient, then some form of unequal opportunity is necessary to achieve equality of result. If freedom is not enough, restrictions on the freedom of some are necessary for the advancement of others—those who came to be known in affirmative action parlance as "specially protected classes" or "preferred classes." Courts and administrative agencies set about implementing this interpretation of equal rights, which now was said to require racial classifications in order to succeed. The watchword of this vision of civil rights was class rights rather than individual rights.

The racial genie, finally having been confined by powerful legal restraints in the Civil Rights Act of 1964, was released again. Many believed that the genie had changed its nature and could be employed as a force for good. That was naive and dangerous. The racial genie tells us to forget the principles of the Declaration. It insists that race is not accidental, but an essential feature of the human persona. It urges us to embrace race openly and honestly—to make it the basis for an administrative state that promises genuine racial progress. Yet, anyone with the slightest acquaintance with human history knows that this siren song presages only evil in the guise of progress.

## Class Rights?

There is no way to say that rights belong to classes without discarding the notion that the first object of civil society is the equal protection of equal rights. If rights belong to classes and not to individuals, then equal protection of the laws is impossible. Class considerations abstract from the individual and ascribe to him or her class characteristics that are different— and necessarily unequal—from those of individuals outside the class. Class claims are claims of inequality, not equality. Likewise, class remedies, such as affirmative action and racial set-asides, assume that all members of the "monolithic white majority" are guilty of racial class injuries and all members of "discrete and insular" minorities are victims of such injuries. This is pure fiction, of course. As Justice Clarence Thomas noted in his concurring opinion in the 1995 case of *Missouri v. Jenkins*. "It goes without saying that only individuals can suffer from discrimination, and only individuals can receive the remedy." Class redresses will afford benefits to some who have not been injured and trammel the rights of some who have not perpetrated injuries. This lack of correspondence between rights and remedies violates the rule of law by making the assignment of rights and remedies simply arbitrary. . . .

### *Gratz v. Bollinger*

In *Gratz v. Bollinger*, one of the two affirmative action decisions handed down in 2003, the Supreme Court struck down

# A Dream Deferred

Three years ago, a bare majority of the Supreme Court of the United States further delayed Dr. Martin Luther King's dream that his children would one day live in a nation where they would "not be judged by the color of their skin but by the content of their character" when five justices ruled colleges and universities could admit students based on their race. . . .

But, on Monday, a new High Court signaled that maybe, just maybe, that same lesson won't be taught to our nation's elementary and high school students. Specifically, the justices agreed to hear two cases next term challenging the practice of some public school districts to use race in deciding whether students can choose to attend the elementary or high school of their choice.

The cases come from Louisville, Kentucky, and Seattle, Washington, where the public school districts allow students (with the assistance of their parents) to choose which schools they want to attend. However, in assigning a school to each student based on his or her preferences, those school districts also considered the student's race if the school of choice already enrolls too many pupils of that same skin color.

Of course, the school districts claim they have a legitimate reason for engaging in this obvious racial discrimination. . . .

In truth, the racial balancing engaged in by the Louisville and Seattle public school districts is anything but permissible under both the Fourteenth Amendment and the Supreme Court's interpretation of it.

*Center for Individual Freedom,*
*"Another Chance for a Colorblind Constitution,"*
CFIF.org Latest News, *June 9, 2006. www.cfif.org.*

the University of Michigan's undergraduate affirmative action admissions program for employing a racial quota. Writing for the majority, Chief Justice William Rehnquist reasoned that the admissions policy, "which automatically distributes 20 points, or one-fifth of the points needed to guarantee admission, to every single 'underrepresented minority' applicant solely because of race, is not narrowly tailored to achieve the interest in educational diversity that [the University] claim[s] justifies [its] program." (One ingredient of strict scrutiny analysis is that even if there is a compelling state interest in considering race, the use of racial classifications must be minimal or "narrowly tailored.") Rehnquist, it is worth noting, did not concede in this opinion that the University had a compelling interest in promoting racial diversity. It was not necessary in *Gratz* to address that question because it was clear that the University operated a quota system that was not narrowly tailored to achieve its asserted interest.

## Grutter v. Bollinger

Writing for the majority in the companion case, *Grutter v. Bollinger*, O'Connor reached back 25 years for her authority, to an argument made by Justice Lewis Powell in *Bakke*. Powell had argued, based on the First Amendment's protection of "academic freedom," that universities have a unique interest in promoting diversity among students. No other justice in 1978 had joined in this opinion and its authority seemed to be limited. O'Connor was not deterred, though, and asserted that the University of Michigan Law School does indeed have a compelling interest in promoting a diverse student body through racial preferences. She did not attempt to explain the necessity of diversity in law schools, merely deferring to the good faith representations by university officials that it enhances education. Such deference to state actors virtually is unheard of in strict scrutiny analysis—for good and obvious reasons. Still, O'Connor wrote that "universities occupy a special niche in our constitutional tradition," and that equal protection considerations must be subordinated to the privileged constitutional postion. Based on this aspect of her opinion, there is some ground for arguing that the ruling will be limited to educational institutions.

The majority in *Grutter* also held that the Law School admissions policy did not employ a racial quota system, but rather sought to achieve a "critical mass" of "underrepresented minority students." Unlike a "racial quota," a critical mass does not involve "outright racial balancing," which would be "patently unconstitutional." A critical mass is defined as a sufficient number to ensure that "underrepresented minority students do not feel isolated or like spokespersons for their race." (Michigan may not admit minority students for the purpose of having a minority point of view represented, because that would be "impermissible stereotyping." A critical mass only can be used to dispel "racial stereotypes" by demonstrating that there are "a variety of viewpoints among minority students.")

University of Michigan officials said that a critical mass could be anywhere between 12-20% of the student body. Although there is no single fixed number involved, dissenters pointed out that critical mass merely is a quota in disguise. Indeed, Thomas contended that the distinction between the two was "purely sophistic." At any rate, in one of the most bizarre turns in an already strange opinion O'Connor stated that the university could employ these "racial preferences" only for another 25 years. By that time, she claimed, the playing field will have been leveled and preferences no longer will be necessary.

## Racial Entitlement

Forty years ago, skeptics were assured that affirmative action merely was a temporary measure, and that it would end when genuine equal opportunity had been achieved. However, everyone knew—or should have known—that once racial class entitlements are established, they are not abolished easily. Twenty-five years from now, the idea they are based on only will become stronger. There is no self-limiting "termination point" in the regime of racial entitlements.

In a powerful dissent in *Grutter*, Thomas noted that "the Constitution abhors classifications based on race . . . because every time the government places citizens on racial registers and makes race relevant to the provision of burdens or benefits, it demeans us all." Thomas concluded that the majority decision "has placed its imprimatur on a practice the can only weaken the principle of equality embodied in the Declaration of Independence and the Equal Protection Clause." Just so.

> *"For years the federal government has given money to schools, including money for programs that explicitly take race into account in making school assignments, to encourage efforts at integration. And for good reason: Students—and ultimately society—benefit when black children and white go to school together."*

# The Government Should Consider Race in Order to Achieve Integration

*Ruth Marcus*

*In the following 2006 viewpoint, Ruth Marcus criticizes recent Court cases in which the federal government has tried to stop school integration. In these cases the federal government holds that segregation and integration are equally offensive to the Fourteenth Amendment and the concept of equal protection. However, Marcus contends that school integration is beneficial to society and does not involve harmful discrimination. In this case she says, government should be allowed to consider race. Marcus is a columnist for the* Washington Post.

As you read, consider the following questions:

1. According to Jack Greenberg, U.S. justices are being urged to do what?
2. What common characteristics do Seattle's and Louisville's integration plans share?
3. From 1973 to 2000, Louisville was under a court order to do what?

A half-century after *Brown v. Board of Education*, it's come, amazingly, to this: The Supreme Court, in the name of preventing race discrimination, is being asked to stop local schools from voluntarily adopting plans to promote integration.

Even more amazingly, the federal government—a government that sided with the black schoolchildren in *Brown* and has spent years helping enforce the court's desegregation decree—has entered the case on the side of white parents challenging the plans.

Thurgood Marshall must be spinning in his grave.

## Fourteenth Amendment and Equal Protection Make Integration Difficut

This perverse notion of constitutional rights would mean that the guarantee of equal protection makes it harder, not easier, to integrate schools. As Jack Greenberg, Marshall's co-counsel in *Brown*, put it in a recent friend-of-the-court brief, the justices are being urged "to hold, in effect, that integration and segregation are equally offensive to the Fourteenth Amendment insofar as they involve any consideration of race."

It's a measure of how far we have come from the lessons and promise of *Brown*, and how inured we have become to a Justice Department hostile to civil rights, that the administration's intervention in these cases—it will argue before the court on Monday—has not generated more outrage.

# Segregation Is Still Alive

As America's public schools become more segregated in the 21st Century, school boards are attempting to reverse the trend through innovative initiatives to ensure that today's classrooms reflect the diversity of the communities in which we live. This term [Oct. 2006–Oct. 2007] the U.S. Supreme Court will hear voluntary integration cases from Seattle, WA and Louisville, KY (*Parents Involved in Community Schools v. Seattle School District* and *Meredith v. Jefferson County Board of Education*) that will determine if local school boards will be permitted to foster racially and ethnically diverse public schools in their communities.

Fifty-two years after the *Brown v. Board of Education* decision outlawed school segregation, the Court will consider whether America can continue to work towards the promise of that landmark ruling. Voluntary integration plans are the last remaining measures available to school districts to fulfill the *Brown* mandate to integrate the nation's public schools.

*NAACP Legal Defense Fund, "LDF Urges Court to Reaffirm Equal Education for All Children," LDF Cases: Latest Developments, October 18, 2006. www.naacpldf.org.*

Public schools are less integrated today than they were in 1970. In the South, many school systems, once segregated by law, have been freed from court oversight and, with the return to neighborhood schools, have reverted to their former state. The percentage of black children attending schools that are mostly minority increased from 66 percent in 1991 to 73 percent in 2003, according to the Harvard Civil Rights Project.

# Promoting Integration Is Not Discriminatory

Communities trying to do better than this should be celebrated, not sued.

The cases before the court involve school systems in Seattle and Louisville. Their plans differ—Seattle's affected only high school assignments, Louisville's involved elementary through high school—but they share common characteristics: They offer children a choice of schools and give weight to factors such as geographic proximity and sibling attendance. Race comes up only when a particular school's racial balance is far out of line with the city's student body as a whole.

This is not the kind of invidious discrimination that is at the core of the Supreme Court's aversion to racial classifications. As federal appeals court Judge Alex Kozinski, a Reagan appointee, wrote in the Seattle case: "No race is turned away from government service or services. The plan does not segregate the races; to the contrary, it seeks to promote integration. There is no attempt to give members of particular races political power based on skin color. There is no competition between the races, and no race is given a preference over another. That a student is denied the school of his choice may be disappointing, but it carries no racial stigma and says nothing at all about that individual's aptitude or ability."

Strikingly, Louisville was under court order to remedy intentional segregation in its schools from 1973 until 2000—at which point the Clinton Justice Department, arguing that the system hadn't yet eradicated the traces of its former discriminatory system, opposed freeing the district from court supervision.

Now President Bush's Justice Department argues against giving Louisville flexibility to ensure that its schools don't spring back to their previous state of racial isolation. Under this upside-down logic, a school system that is under court order one day to use race-based remedies finds itself barred the next day from doing anything race-based to prevent its schools from reverting to segregated patterns. What happened to respect for local control of schools?

## Sometimes Considering Race Has Merit

The administration's position flies in the face of five decades of federal education policy, enshrined most recently in the No Child Left Behind law. For years the federal government has given money to schools, including money for programs that explicitly take race into account in making school assignments, to encourage efforts at integration.

And for good reason: Students—and ultimately society—benefit when black children and white go to school together. These cases don't present the harder, zero-sum issues of affirmative action; no one's being denied admission. Indeed, creating more integrated public schools could help bring about the day when affirmative action in higher education is no longer critical to ensuring a diverse student body.

There are grounds for nervousness about what the court is up to. Justice Sandra Day O'Connor, the fifth vote to uphold affirmative action in higher education, is gone; two new conservative justices are on the court. The justices reached out to take the cases even though all three circuits that have considered the issue upheld the constitutionality of such plans.

What's needed here is a dollop of Kozinskian common sense—for the court to approve an approach that, in the judge's words, "gives the American melting pot a healthy stir without benefitting or burdening any particular group." The Supreme Court shouldn't take away the school systems' spoon.

| "The victim must see that, although oth-
ers have wronged him, his fate lies in
his own hands."

# Government Cannot Fix the Inequalities Caused by Discrimination Against Blacks

*Amy L. Wax*

*In the following viewpoint, Amy L. Wax declares that only blacks
can heal the scars of slavery and oppression. Although justice
might require society or the government to undo racial harms,
Wax believes true healing can only come from insights and
change within the black community. The government must do
what it can to eliminate racial disadvantage, says Wax, but
blacks must realize that their fate lies in their own hands. Wax is
a professor of law at the University of Pennsylvania Law School.*

As you read, consider the following questions:

1. What is the central tenet of the law of remedies?
2. According to Wax, what are the current barriers to racial equality?
3. What is reverse causation?

Bill Cosby's repeated suggestion that the behavior of some America blacks impedes group progress has transgressed the long-standing taboo against "blaming the victim." Defined by sociologist William Ryan in 1971 as an attempt to explain inequality "by finding defects in the victims of inequality," victim-blaming is virtually banned from polite discourse. The time has come for that to change.

The disdain for anything that smacks of blaming the victim is based on a fundamental confusion. No one can deny that black Americans have endured a history of sustained and grievous mistreatment. Those wrongs have wreaked immeasurable harm. The key question confronting society is not how the harms occurred. Rather, the crucial issue is how to reverse them.

## Law of Remedies: Healing the Victim

A central tenet of the law of remedies is that someone who harms another person—the wrongdoer—must undo that harm. Justice requires that the culprit right the wrong by restoring the victim to his rightful position—the state he would have enjoyed had he never been wronged. In distinguishing between liability and remedy—between causing harm and undoing harm—the law also recognizes that reality can fall short of the ideal. The wrongdoer may quite literally lack the power to make the victim whole. The assailant cannot replace the eye he has destroyed. The murderer cannot bring the dead to life. Full justice for the victim may simply be out of reach.

There is a special case in which the victim's injuries can be healed—but not, unfortunately, by the culpable party. Rather, in a cruel twist of fate, the victim is the only one who can wholly undo the harm he has suffered from others' wrongful actions. The victim must restore himself to the rightful position.

Consider the parable of the paraplegic. A reckless driver runs over a pedestrian, leaving him unable to walk. The driver pays for the pedestrian's treatment and physical therapy, but recovery will require a long, exhausting, and painful effort. The victim is angry. It's not his fault, so why must he face an overwhelming, uphill struggle? But there is no help for it. Although the driver can and must pay, he cannot guarantee success. He cannot make his victim walk again.

## The Destructive Legacy of Racism

The parable illuminates the present dilemma of black disadvantage. There is no question that the social problems blacks face today are the outgrowth of slavery and gross oppression. Unfortunately, centuries of bias have distorted the victims' behavior and values. Bad habits take on a life of their own, impeding the ability to grasp widening opportunities as society progresses, discrimination abates, and old obstacles fall away. The victim himself has changed in ways that place him beyond the reach of outside help alone.

Enduring injuries to human capital are now the most destructive legacy of racism. Evidence suggests that soft behavioral factors, including low educational attainment, poor socialization and work habits, paternal abandonment, family disarray, and non-marital childbearing, now loom larger than overt exclusion as barriers to racial equality. But society's power to address these patterns is severely limited. Short of outright coercion, it is literally impossible for the government or outsiders to change dysfunctional behavior or make good choices for individuals. No one can force a person to obey the law, study hard, develop useful skills, be well-mannered, speak and write well, work steadily, marry and stay married, be a devoted husband and father, and refrain from bearing children he cannot or will not support. These decisions belong to individuals and families.

## Myth of Reverse Causation

The quest for justice blinds us to these hard truths, fueling the demand that those who created the problem solve it. Because

## Bill Cosby Speaks

Ladies and gentlemen, I really have to ask you to seriously consider what you've heard, and now this is the end of the evening so to speak. I heard a prize fight manager say to his fellow who was losing badly, "David, listen to me. It's not what's he's doing to you. It's what you're not doing."

Ladies and gentlemen, these people set—they opened the doors, they gave us the right, and today, ladies and gentlemen, in our cities and public schools we have fifty percent drop out. In our own neighborhood, we have men in prison. No longer is a person embarrassed because they're pregnant without a husband. No longer is a boy considered an embarrassment if he tries to run away from being the father of the unmarried child.

Ladies and gentlemen, the lower economic and lower middle economic people are not holding their end in this deal. In the neighborhood that most of us grew up in, parenting is not going on. In the old days, you couldn't hooky school because every drawn shade was an eye. And before your mother got off the bus and to the house, she knew exactly where you had gone, who had gone into the house, and where you got on whatever you had one and where you got it from. Parents don't know that today.

I'm talking about these people who cry when their son is standing there in an orange suit. Where were you when he was two? Where were you when he was twelve? Where were you when he was eighteen, and how come you don't know he had a pistol? And where is his father, and why don't you know where he is? And why doesn't the father show up to talk to this boy?

*Bill Cosby, "50th Anniversary of Brown v. Board of Education," speech, May 17, 2004. www.americanrhetoric.com.*

the ideal is that society should fix what's broken, everyone wants to believe society can. Indeed, it is often assumed that everything can be made right just by reversing course. If discrimination is the culprit, then eliminating it is the cure. If racism is to blame, purging racism will do the trick. This is the myth of reverse causation.

## Four Insights for Healing

The law recognizes that reverse causation doesn't always work. Liability may diverge from remedy. The one who caused the problem cannot necessarily solve it. That something is fair does not mean that it is possible. Others can help, but there are some things people can only do for themselves. What do these insights mean for thinking about racial inequality?

First, accepting a key role for victims does not really "blame the victim" because it implies no exoneration of the wrongdoer. Slavery and discrimination, not blacks themselves, brought us to the current predicament. That means that the government must do what it can to eliminate racial disadvantage. Given the nature of the problem, however, its role is necessarily modest. The key reforms must come from within individuals and communities.

True racial justice may not be achievable. Is it fair to charge blacks with the weighty task of self-improvement when others' wrongs have made their burden so great? The answer must be no. But that doesn't change reality. Just as the careless driver can bankroll recovery but cannot make the paraplegic walk again, the government and society can supply resources and create opportunities but cannot return blacks to their rightful place. Try as they might, they cannot fully restore the victims' capacities. Only the victim can heal himself.

Third, rehearsing the history of racial oppression, although important for moral clarity, is of little use in addressing current inequalities. In seeking solutions, we must look forward rather than dwell on the past because the way out of the present dilemma may not resemble the path in. Trial and error, aided by an open mind and a willingness to do what works, should be the order of the day. Above all, the road to true equality begins at home.

Finally, the persistence of racial disadvantage does not mean that society has failed to do enough. The greatest need at present may not be more government spending and new programs but a conversion experience. The victim must see that, although others have wronged him, his fate lies in his own hands. Justice may be forever elusive, but success is the best revenge.

> *"Unfortunately, rather than reducing unfair racial disparities in federal sentencing, the evidence shows that the guidelines made the problem worse."*

# Sentencing Guidelines such as Mandatory Minimum Sentences Are Discriminatory

*John Lewis and Robert Wilkins*

*In the following viewpoint, John Lewis and Robert Wilkins argue that mandatory federal sentencing guidelines created in the 1980s are discriminatory toward blacks. Since the guidelines were enacted, the difference in prison sentences between blacks and whites increased by a wide margin—with blacks getting more prison time on average than whites. Lewis and Wilkins wrote this viewpoint one month before the U.S. Supreme Court handed down a decision—in the* Booker *and* FanFan *cases— that changed the guidelines from mandatory to advisory: judges should consider the guidelines but are not forced to institute them.*

John Lewis and Robert Wilkins, "Fix Sentencing Guidelines: Move to End Disparity along Racial Lines Hasn't Worked," *Atlanta Journal-Constitution*, December 16, 2004. Reproduced by permission of the authors.

As you read, consider the following questions:

1. What was the goal of the U.S. Sentencing Commission when it was created in 1984?

2. What is the difference between the average prison sentence for white offenders versus black offenders in 1984? In 2001?

3. Mandatory minimum drug sentences require powder cocaine defendants to traffic how much more cocaine before they receive the same sentence as crack cocaine defendants?

Any day now, the U.S. Supreme Court is expected to announce its decision in the *Booker* and *FanFan*[1] cases, which raise the issue of whether the federal sentencing guidelines violate the Sixth Amendment right to have a jury determine those facts that can increase the length of any potential sentence.

## Supposed to End Racial Disparities

Many are hoping that the Supreme Court will strike down the guidelines, which have been lambasted by a diverse group of judges, practitioners and academics. Others are urging the court to uphold the guidelines, and they are preparing quick legislative "fixes" that would allow Congress to keep the present guidelines largely intact should the court strike them down.

Before the enactment of the guidelines, federal judges could consider a broad range of evidence and impose the sentence they believed most appropriate in each case. When Congress created the U.S. Sentencing Commission in 1984, its principal (and laudable) goal was to draft guidelines that eliminated discriminatory sentencing disparities. This approach initially appealed to minority communities because of its promise to sentence everyone fairly.

1. Under the federal sentencing guidelines, *Booker* and *FanFan* each received unusually long prison sentences for drug charges. The subsequent appeals challenged the guidelines as being unconstitutional, taking their cases all the way to the U.S. Supreme Court.

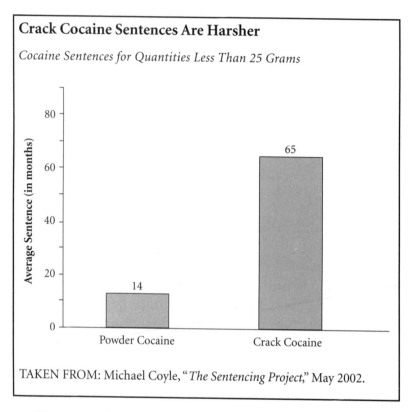

**Crack Cocaine Sentences Are Harsher**

*Cocaine Sentences for Quantities Less Than 25 Grams*

TAKEN FROM: Michael Coyle, "*The Sentencing Project*," May 2002.

However, the guidelines, along with mandatory minimum drug sentences enacted by Congress since 1984, have been roundly criticized as unduly harsh, unduly rigid, removing too much discretion from judges and shifting too much power to prosecutors. The prestigious American College of Trial Lawyers (a group that includes several prominent former federal prosecutors) recently [as of 2004] urged Congress to abolish the current guidelines, calling them "an experiment that has failed."

## Unjust

Indeed, several federal judges have resigned, in whole or in part because of their disgust with the guidelines. The latest was Judge Robert Cindrich of Pittsburgh, who said last February, "When the law provides a result that is repugnant, we must still follow the law. . . . And you can only do that so many times before you start to wonder, 'How many more times am I going to put my name on this sentence that I don't believe in?'"

One such example of unjust sentencing is Kemba Smith. Smith was a first offender who never used, sold or handled drugs and was connected with a crack cocaine ring only through actions done at the behest of her abusive boyfriend. Nonetheless Smith received a 24-year federal sentence, and she won release from prison after six years only because of intense media coverage and a grant of clemency from President Bill Clinton. Most defendants like Smith are not so lucky.

## Increased Racial Disparities

Unfortunately, rather than reducing unfair racial disparities in federal sentencing, the evidence shows that the guidelines made the problem worse. Just before Thanksgiving [November 2004], the Sentencing Commission released a report assessing whether the federal sentencing system has achieved the goals of the 1984 reforms. It confirmed what many observers have long known: In the past 20 years, the federal prison population has gotten significantly darker.

The report also shows that while the average federal prison sentence for black offenders was about five months longer than for whites in 1984, by 2001, the average sentence for blacks was almost 30 months longer. According to the report, at least some of the disparity is because of controversial mandatory minimum drug sentences and guidelines that require powder cocaine defendants (a racially varied group) to traffic 100 times more cocaine before they receive the same sentence as crack cocaine defendants (who are predominantly black).

The report should serve as a catalyst for major discussion about the racial impact of federal sentencing policy, though, to date, it has received scant attention. Of course, data showing vast racial disparities do not necessarily prove that the federal sentencing system discriminates.

## They Failed

But a critical goal of the federal sentencing guidelines was to eliminate unfair racial disparities in sentencing, and the Sentencing Commission has now concluded that "the sentencing guidelines and mandatory minimum statutes have a greater adverse impact on black offenders than did the factors taken into account by judges in the discretionary system in place immediately prior to guidelines implementation."

Racial disparity in incarceration has been a moral blight on America from the beginning days of our criminal justice system. That this disparity continues despite (and indeed because of) the guidelines highlights the need for serious thinking and action on the issue.

Regardless of whether the Supreme Court strikes them down in the Booker and FanFan cases, Congress should repeal the federal sentencing guidelines along with the mandatory minimum drug sentences. Then, Congress should allow the Sentencing Commission to draft new guidelines that treat the minority community fairly. The experiment with the federal sentencing guidelines has failed—it's time to go back to the drawing board.

| "Federal sentencing guidelines have helped keep Americans safe while also delivering on their promise to reduce unwarranted disparities in sentences."

# Sentencing Guidelines Are Fair and Have Decreased Crime

*Alberto Gonzales*

*In the following viewpoint, Alberto Gonzalez argues that the mandatory sentencing guidelines established by the 1984 Sentencing Reform Act are achieving the desired goals. They are tough, fair, and crime is generally lower. Since the guidelines became advisory in 2005, Gonzalez notes a troubling trend: there is an increase in the number of unusually low sentences. He believes the advisory guidelines must be improved. Gonzalez served as the U.S. attorney general from 2005 to 2007.*

As you read, consider the following questions:

1. What did the Supreme Court rule in January 2005?
2. According to Gonzales, the federal sentencing guidelines were the result of what?
3. Under the advisory guidelines, judges are free to do what?

Alberto Gonzales, "Sentencing Guidelines," speech, U.S. Department of Justice, June 21, 2005. www.usdoj.gov.

Important policies designed to ensure the vindication of victims' rights in federal criminal cases have been developed during the Bush Administration. Last year [2004], the President signed the Justice For All Act. I [subsequently] revised and reissued the Attorney General Guidelines For Victim and Witness Assistance.

## *Mandatory* Guidelines Ensured Tough but Fair Sentences

For victims, another key aspect of any fair and equitable criminal justice system is to ensure that those convicted of crimes serve tough and fair sentences. And since 1987, we have had a sentencing system for federal offenses that responded to this demand—and has helped to achieve the lowest crime rates in a generation.

The key to this system was a set of mandatory sentencing guidelines that specified a range within which federal judges were bound to impose sentences, absent unusual circumstances. The guidelines reflected a careful balancing by Congress and the Sentencing Commission between discretion and consistency in sentencing. But the mandatory guidelines system is no longer in place today, and I believe its loss threatens the progress we have made in ensuring tough and fair sentences for federal offenders.

## Guidelines Became *Advisory* Only

That threat is illustrated by the story of two defendants, both convicted of similar charges involving possession of child pornography, one in New York, the other across the Hudson River in New Jersey.

The New York defendant faced a sentencing range of 27 to 33 months in prison, but received only probation.

The New Jersey defendant faced a sentencing range of 30 to 37 months and was given a sentence of 41 months in prison.

What made the difference?

This past January [2005], the Supreme Court ruled that federal sentencing guidelines mandated by bipartisan congressional majorities in 1984 are advisory only and are no longer binding on federal judges.

In that case, *U.S. v. Booker*, the Court held that federal sentencing guidelines violated a defendant's rights under the Sixth Amendment of our Constitution. The result is that, today, judges must take the guidelines into account when sentencing, but are no longer bound by the law to impose a sentence within the range prescribed by the guidelines.

So in the New Jersey child pornography case, the judge deemed it necessary to protect the public from the defendant and imposed a sentence slightly above the guideline range. In the New York case, however, the judge reasoned that the defendant would benefit from continued psychological treatment and ordered probation only.

The story of these two defendants is just one example that illustrates a developing trend in the aftermath of the *Booker* decision. More and more frequently, judges are exercising their discretion to impose sentences that depart from the carefully considered ranges developed by the U.S. Sentencing Commission. In the process, we risk losing a sentencing system that requires serious sentences for serious offenders and helps prevent disparate sentences for equally serious crimes.

And why, you may be asking, should victims and victims' groups be concerned about sentencing?

## 1984 Sentencing Reform Act

The federal sentencing guidelines were the result of Republicans and Democrats coming together in response to the high crime rates of the 1960s and 1970s to create an invaluable tool of justice.

As the rates of serious violent felonies more than tripled, a consensus emerged that society needed to be protected from the early release of offenders.

Also undermining Americans' faith in the system was the fact that significant disparities existed in the sentences received by individuals guilty of equally serious offenses.

A widespread and bipartisan consensus took hold that our system of sentencing was unfair and broken.

So in 1984, lawmakers from across the political spectrum passed the Sentencing Reform Act with two broad goals in mind.

The first was to increase the safety of law-abiding Americans by restoring in sentencing an emphasis on punishment, incapacitation, and deterrence.

The second was to ensure fairness in sentencing. The statute's guiding principle was consistency—defendants who had committed equally serious crimes and had similar criminal backgrounds should receive similar sentences, irrespective of their race or the race of their victim and irrespective of geographic location or economic background.

## Mandatory Guidelines Worked

In the 17-plus years that they have been in existence, federal sentencing guidelines have achieved the ambitious goals of public safety and fairness set out by Congress.

The United States is today [as of 2005] experiencing crime rates that are the lowest in a generation. If crime rates during the last 10 years had been as high as the rates 30–40 years ago, then 34 million additional violent crimes would have been committed in the last decade.

Of course, no single law or policy is by itself responsible for today's low levels of violent crime. But multiple, independent studies of our criminal justice system confirm what our common sense tells us: increased incarceration means reduced crime, and federal and state sentencing reform has helped put

## The *Booker* Mess

Each year, over 65,000 criminal defendants are sentenced in the federal courts; about 1,200 are sentenced each week. Since 1984, Congress has required sentences to be determined according to a strict and detailed set of Sentencing Guidelines. On January 12, 2005, in *United States v. Booker*, the Supreme Court declared this sentencing system unconstitutional. The Justices left many questions unanswered regarding how the lower courts should treat defendants sentenced under the prior regime and how to sentence defendants in the future. These issues occupied much of the attention of federal courts during 2005. The Tenth Circuit alone rendered two en banc decisions and some 226 panel decisions (as of this writing), addressing how to deal with defendants who were sentenced before *Booker* was decided. Nationwide, this retrospective question produced a four-way circuit split and literally thousands of panel decisions. And it will require many more decisions to figure out how to apply *Booker* moving forward.

*Judge Michael W. McConnell,*
*"The* Booker *Mess," Denver University Law Review,*
*vol. 83, no. 3, 2006, p. 665. www.law.du.edu/lawreview.*

the most violent, repeat offenders behind bars, and kept them there for sentences appropriate to their crimes.

Federal sentencing guidelines have helped keep Americans safe while also delivering on their promise to reduce unwarranted disparities in sentences. When the U.S. Sentencing Commission recently took stock of 15 years experience with the federal sentencing guidelines, it noted that studies by both the Commission itself and others have determined that the guidelines, quote, "have succeeded at the job they were principally designed to do: reduce unwarranted disparity arising from differences among judges."

For 17 years, mandatory federal sentencing guidelines have helped drive down crime. The guidelines have evolved over time to adapt to changing circumstances and a better understanding of societal problems and the criminal justice system. Judges, legislators, the Sentencing Commission, prosecutors, defense lawyers, and others have worked hard to develop a system of sentencing guidelines that has protected Americans and improved American justice.

## Advisory Guidelines Worrisome

I am concerned, however, that, under an advisory guidelines system, we will not be able to sustain this progress and victims may be victimized once again by a system that is intended to protect them.

And not because judges aren't doing their best in each and every case. Deciding the fate of a defendant is a serious and difficult task, and our judges discharge this obligation conscientiously and with integrity. As a former judge, I know well the difficulties of the task and I admire the men and women on our federal bench. But it is inevitable over time that, with so many different individual judges involved, exercising their own individual discretion, in so many different jurisdictions, shorter sentences and disparities among sentences will occur under a system of advisory guidelines.

And, indeed, the evidence the Department has seen since the *Booker* decision suggests an increasing disparity in sentences, and a drift toward lesser sentences.

Moreover, our U.S. Attorneys consistently report that a critical law enforcement tool has been taken from them. Under the sentencing guidelines, defendants were only eligible to receive reductions in sentences in exchange for cooperation when the government petitioned the court. Under the advisory guidelines system, judges are free to reduce sentences when they believe the defendant has sufficiently cooperated. And since defendants no longer face penalties that are serious and certain, key witnesses are increasingly less inclined to cooperate with prosecutors. We risk a return to the pre-guidelines era, when defendants were encouraged to "play the odds" in our criminal justice system, betting that the luck of the draw—the judge randomly assigned to their case—might result in a lighter sentence.

## Troubling Trend

In one recent [as of 2005] case, a South Carolina man pled guilty to federal weapons and drug trafficking charges. The firearms in his possession included a fully automatic machine gun, two assault rifles, and two pistols. After his arrest on these charges, this defendant was released on bond. While out on bond, he failed a drug test and absconded from electronic monitoring. Federal marshals caught up with him and, after a six-hour standoff, tear-gassed him out of the house where he was hiding. Under the federal sentencing guidelines, this individual, who had a long history of state charges related to assault and drug possession, faced up to 27 years in prison. However, post-*Booker*, the judge sentenced him to only 10, offering no explanation. The Department is appealing this unreasonably low sentence.

In other cases, defendants are receiving sentences dramatically lower than the guidelines range without any explanation, or on the basis of factors that could not be considered under the guidelines.

In a case involving white collar crime, a Kansas rancher got 1.8 million dollars in cattle loans, falsely claiming that he was using the money to buy live cattle. He even took bank officials to livestock pens and claimed that the cows he was showing them were purchased with loan proceeds, when, in fact he lost all the money speculating on the cattle futures market. He pled guilty to defrauding the bank and faced a sentencing range of 37 to 46 months under the guidelines. But the judge gave him probation only, reasoning, in part, that the defendant had suffered enough when the bank foreclosed on his house.

We have also seen how a system without mandatory guidelines led to a radically reduced sentence for a previously convicted felon convicted of evading federal taxes.

This New York defendant was sentenced in 2003 for evading the payment of more than six million dollars in taxes by such means as moving out of the country valuable assets—including a fleet of Rolls Royces. Under the then-mandatory sentencing guidelines, the defendant was sentenced to 41 months in prison. The judge said he would have liked to impose a considerably lesser sentence, but felt constrained by the guidelines.

A year and half later, after the *Booker* decision, the defendant petitioned the court for re-sentencing and the judge reduced his sentence to seven months in prison and seven months of home confinement. The judge noted that the defendant's age and the need to take care of his wife—not normally relevant sentencing factors pre-*Booker*—now justified a lesser sentence.

The trend suggested by these examples is consistent with the statistics being compiled by the U.S. Sentencing Commission. According to the Commission, sentencing within the guidelines by federal judges has fallen from almost 70 percent in 2003 to under 63 percent today. This trend is troubling to me and should be troubling to all victims of crime.

After reviewing the data, consulting with our prosecutors in the field, and reaching out to other interested parties, I have come to the conclusion that the advisory guidelines system we currently have can and must be improved.

| "Supporting the letter and spirit of Title IX has made life better at our institutions for both women and men."

# Title IX Is a Success and Should Not Be Blamed for Hurting Men's Sports

## Jo Young Switzer

*In this viewpoint, Jo Young Switzer asserts that Title IX, the federal law which prevents gender-based discrimination in educational programs, is quietly working at smaller colleges across the nation. Switzer says at smaller colleges there are no complaints that Title IX is hurting men's sports—an opinion generally heard at high-profile Division I colleges. At smaller colleges, coaches and athletic directors of both men's and women's sports work together to achieve Title IX's goals of expanding women's opportunities and creating equity between men's and women's sports. Switzer became president of Manchester College in North Manchester, IN, on July 1, 2005.*

Jo Young Switzer, "Reflections on Title IX: A Voice from Division III," *On Campus with Women*, Association of American Colleges and Universities, spring/summer 2003, vol. 32, nos. 3–4. www.aacu.org/ocww. Copyright © 2003 by the Association of American Colleges and Universities. Reprinted with permission from *On Campus with Women*.

As you read, consider the following questions:

1. According to Switzer, since Title IX began how many more women participate in college sports?
2. According to Switzer, what is one of the most harmful unintended consequences of Title IX?
3. How can athletic programs with disproportionate participation numbers comply with Title IX?

Too often, media coverage of the debates about Title IX only look at high profile, highly competitive Division I institutions. And they typically do so by paying undue attention to a group upset by a cancellation of a men's team. In doing so, they obscure the quieter revolution that is occurring at NCAA [National Collegiate Athletic Association] Division III schools where the positive influence of Title IX is palpable. These smaller campuses, like my own institution, Manchester College, tell an important part of the story, too often ignored.

## Expansion of Opportunity

Campuses where gender equity is healthiest are those where athletic directors and coaches authentically support Title IX. The impetus behind the development of Title IX was the expansion of opportunities for students, and it has achieved that dream. On our campus, support for gender equity and the overarching goals of Title IX is firm. The support is not expressed in vague clichés. Instead, coaches have demonstrated it in their actions. Ten years ago, Manchester College added two women's teams, but budget freezes made it extremely difficult to find the start up funds needed for equipment, uniforms, and coaches. In response, coaches from other sports voluntarily reallocated funds to meet this need; and when the football coach realized that the budgets were still $3,000 short, he offered even more. As a result, all of the teams were still able to compete. No one complained.

## Title IX, Education Amendments of 1972

Section 1681. Sex

(a) Prohibition against discrimination; exceptions. No person in the United States shall, on the basis of sex, excluded from participation in, be denied the benefits of, or be subjected to discrimination under any education program or activity receiving Federal financial assistance.

*Title IX Patsy T. Mink Equal Opportunity in Education Act,
20 U.S.C. § 1681. www.access.gpo.gov/uscode/index.html.*

Only thirty years after Title IX began, five times more women participate in college sports than before, and some will become future coaches. Title IX has already produced many of the women who are now coaches. Each woman coach of a varsity sport on our campus succeeds in part because Title IX opened doors for her through her own college athletic participation. This is true of the majority of women coaches in colleges today. Continued athletic opportunities for women will allow them to be actively involved in collegiate competition, interested in athletic internships, and qualified, in time, for head coaching positions. Everyone benefits when the best people are coaches, and Title IX ensures an excellent training ground for those coaches.

## Equity Between Men's and Women's Sports

Equity between men's and women's sports also means that coaches will have more mentors. On our campus, men and women coaches discuss game strategies and practice protocols. One coach can help another learn to run a good practice session, regardless of whether it is a men's or a women's sport, or whether it is a male or a female coach. A good practice session is a good practice session. Male coaches mentor female coaches and vice versa.

The success of Title IX shows up in many other ways not captured by the often-quoted proportionality numbers. Title IX itself does not have a quota system, nor does it require exact proportionality of money and numbers of sports. One of the most harmful unintended consequences of Title IX has been the focus only on proportionality because it is the easiest to measure. Title IX has never been about limiting participation: it has been primarily about expanding opportunities.

Title IX allows schools to decide what teams they will offer, both men's and women's. Athletic programs with disproportionate participation numbers can still comply with Title IX as long as other measures of equity—progress and interest—are present. On our campus, like many other campuses, having a football program makes it very hard to have exactly the same numbers of male and female athletes. We do, however, ensure that the funding we allocate for athletics is the same per athlete for all sports—both men's and women's. We ensure that coaching assignments and pay are equitable. We ensure that practice times are assigned so that every player—male or female—has the pleasure of practicing at 5 a.m. when the practice facility is busy from 5 a.m. through 1 a.m. during the winter months. We are also developing ways to get a more accurate understanding of student interest in athletic participation.

## Oversimplifications

The belief that Title IX hurts men's sports oversimplifies a very complex situation. Schools with limited resources cut sports for many different reasons. Gender equity is just one factor in those decisions. Media continue to focus on elimination of wrestling at high-visibility universities even though, nationwide, wrestling numbers are increasing. In fact, men's participation in college athletics overall has increased since Title IX began. The bottom line is that schools can maintain many athletic teams if they are willing to allocate smaller budgets to the teams. On campuses like ours, where the athletic leaders and the coaches are willing to allocate resources so that more students can participate, the system works.

## Measures of Success

Historically, athletic playing fields have been the proving grounds for several cultural changes in the U.S. Professional baseball, for instance, shattered the accepted racial segregation of the period. Title IX has likewise disrupted the gender norms of our day. Supporting the letter and spirit of Title IX has made life better at our institutions for both women and men. One measure of success is that we have more women and men student athletes than ever before. And they admire and support each other. Football players cheer for the softball team at the conference tournament. The women's soccer team cheers on the men's cross country team.

Title IX is still maturing. Just imagine how many more changes in men's and women's lives we have yet to witness.

> "The program [Title IX] has transformed into having the reverse effect on men's sports, which have experienced budget cuts or have had their programs eliminated all together."

# Title IX Hurts Men's Sports

*Sara Foley*

*In the following viewpoint, Sara Foley says that Title IX has achieved its intended goals and is no longer necessary. Women's sports have grown exponentially, says Foley, to a point where women no longer need the assistance provided in Title IX. Meanwhile, Title IX has been hurting men's sports. As programs try to comply with Title IX, they have been cutting men's sports budgets and eliminating many men's programs. Foley wrote this viewpoint while a student at Texas A&M University.*

As you read, consider the following questions:

1. According to Washingtonpost.com, how many NCAA female athletes were there in 1972? In 2000?
2. Who established a commission to review Title IX practices?
3. What does the three-part test of the original Title IX law involve?

Title IX, a law banning sexual discrimination in collegiate and high school sports, has aided many female athletic departments in getting recognition and funding for teams that might not exist without it. Since its enactment in 1972, women's athletic programs have grown exponentially, from less than 30,000 NCAA female athletes in 1972 to almost 151,000 in 2000, according to Washingtonpost.com. From the perspective of women athletes, coaches, supporters and equality activists, this program has forced universities and secondary schools to provide women and men with the same opportunities, as well as assuring that women's interests are being met.

However, there are two sides to every story. Title IX is far from flawless, as many under-funded male athletes will attest to. The program has transformed into having the reverse effect on men's sports, which have experienced budget cuts or have had their programs eliminated all together, while women's sports have grown in numbers and funding without a significant increase in student interest. The law may have been necessary in 1972, but with the advances it has made, it is no longer needed. Changes are needed to comply with the strong force of women's sports that does not need its foot in the door, as it did 31 years ago.

Men's teams have certainly noticed the injustice this law has brought about. The National Wrestling Coaches Association filed a lawsuit last year, protesting the significant amount of wrestling programs cut to comply with equality figures stated in Title IX. This, along with many other complaints, caused Education Secretary Roderick R. Paige to establish a commission to review the current Title IX practices and to possibly dilute the strength of this contradictory law, according to cnn.com.

The commission, which concluded Jan. 31, [2003] provided Paige with a list of suggestions, most of which were

# Title IX Discrimination Against Men

Johnny has wrestled his whole life, and his senior year, he nearly wins states. He's worked hard to achieve his 4.0 gpa and has participated in a few clubs, all while holding a steady job. He hopes to go to MUU on a full ride that could be offered; he's dreamed of going to this school since the days of his childhood. Unfortunately, he receives a letter in the mail, apologizing for not being able to send him any sort of scholarship, and is declined the opportunity to participate whatsoever. Sue, who isn't very athletic, and hasn't seriously been interested in any sports at all, has never had a job, and is only a C average student, is suggested she apply for an athletics scholarship to MUU. She receives a full ride to play field hockey in a matter of weeks. What we are dealing with is discrimination towards men, induced by Title IX. Thus, Title IX needs an overhaul, and partial removal from sports until it effectively provides all athletes the opportunities they rightly deserve to succeed in sports.

*Kevin Ford, "Title IX—Controversial? Perhaps," K's, May 17, 2005.*
*http://bassguy101.blogspot.com.*

geared at clarifying current procedures. One suggestion is to allow campus surveys to gauge student interest, and to establish programs based on the results. The most controversial change would allow for as little as 43 percent of the varsity slots to be allocated for females, despite the percentage of female students being higher than that, according to Washingtonpost.com. Although these amendments might seem to be taking a step backward, in actuality, they would provide equality instead of a growing preference toward women's sports, an unnatural partiality mandated by law instead of real interest.

The original law involves a three-part test, stating that either the male and female participation in sports must be proportionate to the student body composition, that female athletic opportunities must be added, or by verifying that the interests of women at the school are being met. The result of this has been the continual addition of sports programs for women on college campuses and the elimination of some male programs, due to budget constraints. The law wasn't designed to put males at a disadvantage, according to an interview Paige had with the Washington Post.

Legislation demanding equality will only bring about ineffective results, such as the unnecessary addition of women's programs strictly for the purpose of equality. While Title IX has brought women significant strides in equality, the necessity of the ruling has timed out. Women's sports will continue to grow, with or without legislation to force its growth. Considering the significance women's sports now hold, Title IX will give women aid they don't need at the expense of men. This has already happened on several college campuses, such as Providence College, which was forced to cut three men's sports programs to allow room in the budget for female programs that have drawn little interest, according to cnn.com.

The suggestions raised by the commission head in the right direction ... By adopting a more relaxed attitude toward Title IX enforcement, schools will take steps to achieve equality instead of merely proclaiming compliance with it.

# Periodical Bibliography

The following articles have been selected to supplement the diverse views presented in this chapter.

James P. Anelli and Laura H. Corvo — "The Ever Expanding Discrimination Statutes," *New Jersey Law Journal*, April 10, 2006.

Judith A. Baer — "Women's Rights and the Constitution," *Social Science Journal*, January 1, 2007.

Frank Deford — "Unfair Advantage: Annual Title IX Ax Is About to Fall on Men's Sports," *Sports Illustrated*, May 2, 2007.

Donald B. Holsinger — "Inequality in the Public Provision of Education: Why It Matters," *Comparative Education Review*, August 2005.

Viveca Novak — "10 Questions for Alberto Gonzalez," *Time*, October 2, 2005.

Holona Leanne Ochs — "'Colorblind' Policy in Black and White: Racial Consequences of Disenfranchisement Policy," *Policy Studies Journal*, February 2006.

Bill Penington — "Fair Play?" *New York Times Upfront*, January 15, 2007.

Frederic Rodgers — "Our Constitution Is Color Blind," *Judges Journal*, Spring 2004.

Ron Schachter — "Title IX Turns 35: The Landmark Law Faces a Happy Birthday—and a Midlife Crisis," *University Business*, March 2007.

Gary Smith — "Blindsided by History," *Sports Illustrated*, April 9, 2007.

Floyd D. Weatherspoon — "Racial Justice and Equity for African-American Males in the American Educational System: A Dream Forever Deferred," *North Carolina Central Law Journal*, 2006.

# For Further Discussion

## Chapter 1

1. Both Ishmael Reed's and John McWhorter's viewpoints are based on their own personal experiences. Which account do you think is the most accurate reflection of the middle-class black experience in the early twenty-first century and why?

2. Julian Bond believes that sexual orientation is a condition people are born with and cannot change. Do you think all people who agree with this statement *also* believe as Bond does, that gays should be allowed to marry? Explain. Do you think Timothy J. Dailey agrees or disagrees with this statement?

## Chapter 2

1. Michelle Malkin contends that the chance of preventing a terrorist attack outweighs the negative impacts of discrimination based on racial profiling. The Leadership Conference on Civil Rights Education Fund report authors disagree. Whose argument do you agree with and why? Do you think that Malkin has ever been profiled? Why or why not?

2. The Institute of Medicine believes that minorities receive a different quality of health care than whites because of race or ethnicity. Jonathan Klick and Sally Satel say that the reason minorities receive a different quality of health care is not because of race but because of socioeconomic status. Which viewpoint is based more on statistics and

which viewpoint uses more empirical data? Describe the difference between statistics and empirical data. Do you think one or the other is more persuasive? Why or why not?

3. Do you think, as Nedd Kareiva does, that health care providers are being discriminated against when they are forced to treat people who offend their religious beliefs? Do you think, as Natalie Hope McDonald does, that gays are being discriminated against when they are refused treatment by a doctor or are given anti-gay materials? Is it possible to say yes to both questions? Based on your answers to these questions, do you think all discrimination is the same?

## Chapter 3

1. Do you think the fact that Ward Connerly is black has any impact on his argument? Explain.

2. Why do David L. Chambers, Timothy T. Clydesdale, William C. Kidder, and Richard O. Lempert believe that the benefits of affirmative action outweigh the costs? Why does Richard Sander believe they do not? Whose argument is the most convincing and why?

3. Larry Elders says that Americans would not tolerate quotas in the National Basketball Association (NBA). Do you agree or disagree with this claim and why? Do you think his analogy is relevant? Why or why not?

## Chapter 4

1. Richard Thompson Ford generally thinks that the U.S. legal system is effective in remedying discrimination, while Stephanie M. Wildman believes sometimes the U.S. legal system is ineffective towards discrimination. Do you think the U.S. legal system is efficient in remedying discrimination? Why or why not?

2. Do you believe as Edward Erler does that government should be "color blind" in *every* instance? Or do you believe as Ruth Marcus does that when it is for the greater good, *sometimes* race should be considered? Explain.

3. After reading the viewpoints by John Lewis and Robert Wilkins and Alberto Gonzalez, what do you think are some of the pros and cons of *mandatory* versus *advisory* sentencing guidelines?

4. Do you think Sara Foley would agree with Jo Young Switzer that the perception of Title IX is different at large schools than it is at small schools? Do you think Foley is primarily referring to small or large schools in her viewpoint?

# Organizations to Contact

*The editors have compiled the following list of organizations concerned with the issues debated in this book. The descriptions are derived from materials provided by the organizations. All have publications or information available for interested readers. The list was compiled on the date of publication of the present volume; the information provided here may change. Be aware that many organizations take several weeks or longer to respond to inquiries, so allow as much time as possible.*

**Adversity.Net**
P.O. Box 7099, Silver Spring, MD   20907-7099
e-mail: editor@adversity.net
Web site: www.adversity.net

Adversity.Net is a non-profit, educational organization dedicated to the elimination of racial preferences and quotas. The organization provides information to the public about reverse discrimination and racial preferences and provides a resource and support system for victims of reverse discrimination. The Web site provides links to many articles about reverse discrimination, racial profiling, immigration, reparation and other topics.

**Alliance for Marriage**
P.O. Box 2490, Merrifield, VA   22116
(703) 934-1212 • fax: (703) 934-1211
Web site: www.allianceformarriage.org

The Alliance for Marriage (AFM) is a research and education organization dedicated to protecting the institution of traditional marriage and addressing the epidemic of fatherless families in the United States. AFM educates the public, the media, elected officials, and civil society leaders on the benefits of marriage for children, adults and society. The organization publishes an electronic newsletter.

# American-Arab Anti-Discrimination Committee
4201 Connecticut Avenue, Washington, DC   20008
(202) 244-2990 • fax: (202) 244-3196
e-mail: adc@adc.org
Web site: www.adc.org

The American-Arab Anti-Discrimination Committee (ADC) is a civil rights organization committed to defending the rights of American citizens of Arab descent. The organization combats negative stereotyping of Arab Americans, provides advocacy, analyzes policy, provides education, and has a department of legal services. The organization provides email "action alerts" on numerous issues.

# American Civil Liberties Union
125 Broad Street, 18th Floor, New York, NY   10004
Web site: www.aclu.org

The mission of the American Civil Liberties Union (ACLU) is to preserve and protect the civil rights of all Americans as set forth by the United States Constitution, its amendments, and civil rights statutes. The ACLU works to extend rights to segments of the population that have traditionally been denied their rights, including Native Americans and other people of color; lesbians, gay men, bisexuals and transgendered people; women; mental-health patients; prisoners; people with disabilities; and the poor. The organization's Web site provides many publications such as "Know Your Rights" pamphlets, advocacy materials, flyers, and reports.

# American Civil Rights Institute
P.O. Box 188350, Sacramento, CA   95818
(916) 444-2278 • fax: (916) 444-2279
e-mail: feedback@acri.org
Web site: www.acri.org

The American Civil Rights Institute (ACRI) is a nationally recognized civil rights organization created to educate the public about racial and gender preferences. It was established by Ward Connerly and Dusty Rhodes in 1996. ACRI assists state grassroots organizations and publishes the online newsletter, *The Egalitarian.*

## The Anti-Defamation League
Department: RL, P.O. Box 96226
Washington, DC   20090-6226
(202) 452-8310 • fax: (202) 296-2371
e-mail: washington-dc@adl.org
Web site: www.adl.org

The immediate objective of the Anti-Defamation League (ADL) is to stop the defamation of Jewish people. Its ultimate purpose is to secure justice and fair treatment for all people and to put an end to unfair discrimination against any sect or body of citizens. The organization publishes several newsletters, such as *ADL Connections* and *Headlines.*

## Center for Equal Opportunity
7700 Leesburg Pike, Suite 231, Falls Church, VA   22043
(703) 442-0066 • fax: (703) 442-0449
Web site: www.ceousa.org

The Center for Equal Opportunity (CEO) is a think tank devoted exclusively to the promotion of colorblind equal opportunity and racial harmony. The CEO focuses on three areas in particular: racial preferences, immigration and assimilation, and multicultural education. The organization publishes several reports and articles each year.

## Civil Rights Project
University of California, Los Angeles
8370 Math Sciences
Los Angeles, CA   90095
(310) 267-5562 • fax: (310) 206-6293
e-mail: crp@ucla.edu
Web site: www.civilrightsproject.ucla.edu

The stated mission of the Civil Rights Project is to "help renew the civil rights movement by bridging the worlds of ideas and action." As a resource for information on racial justice, the project convenes national conferences, commissions research, and produces major reports on topics such as desegregation and diversity. The *Civil Rights Project Quarterly Newsletter* is freely available on its Web site.

## Independent Women's Forum
1726 M Street NW 10th Floor
Washington, DC 20036
(202) 419-1820
e-mail: info@iwf.org
Web site: www.iwf.org

The stated mission of the Independent Women's Forum (IWF) is to rebuild civil society by advancing economic liberty, personal responsibility, and political freedom. The organization promotes limited government, equality under the law, and strong families, and generally opposes affirmative action, Title IX, and feminism. IWF experts examine legal, political, domestic, and foreign policy issues, particularly as they pertain to women and provide commentary and analysis. The IWF publishes various articles and special reports annually.

## Leadership Conference on Civil Rights
1629 K Street NW 10th Floor, Washington, DC 20006
(202) 466-3311
Web site: www.civilrights.org

The Leadership Conference on Civil Rights (LCCR), founded in 1950 by three prominent civil rights advocates, seeks to promote equal opportunity and protect civil rights. LCCR maintains the www.civilrights.org Web site, providing socially concerned, issue-oriented audio, video, and written programming. The organization's publication, *Civil Rights Monitor*, is available on a quarterly basis. Additionally, it provides daily or weekly email newsletters and various reports and educational curricula.

## National Association for the Advancement of Colored People
4805 Mt. Hope Drive, Baltimore, MD 21215
(877) NAACP-98 • fax: (202) 463-2953

e-mail: washingtonbureau@naacpnet.org
Web site: www.naacp.org

The National Association for the Advancement of Colored People (NAACP), the nation's oldest civil rights organization, seeks to ensure the equality of rights of all persons and to eliminate racial discrimination in the United States. The organization provides research and advocacy, policy analysis, youth outreach, scholarships, and has a significant legal department. The NAACP distributes several publications, including *The Crisis* and *The Advocate*.

**National Gay and Lesbian Task Force**
1325 Massachusetts Avenue NW, Suite 600
Washington, DC  20005
(202) 393-5177 • fax: (202) 393-2241
e-mail: theTaskForce@TheTaskForce.org
Web site: www.thetaskforce.org

The National Gay and Lesbian Task Force (NGLTF) is an advocacy group working to protect the civil rights of gay, lesbian, bisexual, and transgender people in the United States. The organization works to organize campaigns and train activists at the state and local level to fight the anti-gay and lesbian agenda. The Task Force publishes the magazine *Creating Change* three times each year as well as weekly electronic newsletter, *The Task Force Update*.

**National Organization for Women**
1100 H Street NW, 3rd Floor, Washington, DC  20005
(202) 628-8669 • fax: (202) 785-8576
e-mail: now@now.org
Web site: www.now.org

The National Organization for Women (NOW), the largest organization of feminist activists in the United States, works to eliminate discrimination and harassment against women and promote equality and justice in the United States. NOW advocates for women's rights on a number of issues such as reproductive freedom, lesbian rights, and economic justice. NOW publishes the *National NOW Times* three or four times per year.

# U.S. Equal Employment Opportunity Commission

1801 L Street NW, Washington, DC   20507
(800) 669-4000
e-mail: info@ask.eeoc.gov
Web site: www.eeoc.gov

The Equal Employment Opportunity Commission (EEOC) is a U.S. government agency whose job is to eliminate illegal discrimination from all American workplaces. The organization enforces U.S. anti-discrimination laws and promotes equal opportunity employment. It's Youth@Work initiative is a national education and outreach campaign to promote equal employment opportunity for American youth workers. The organization publishes fact sheets and general information about workplace discrimination.

# Bibliography of Books

David E.
Bernstein

*You Can't Say That! The Growing Threat to Civil Liberties from Antidiscrimination Laws.* Washington, DC: Cato Institute, 2003.

Kevin Boyle

*Arc of Justice: A Saga of Race, Civil Rights, and Murder in the Jazz Age.* New York: Henry Holt, 2004.

Martha Burk

*Cult of Power: Sex Discrimination in Corporate America and What Can Be Done About It.* New York: Scribner, 2005.

George Chauncey

*Why Marriage? The History Shaping Today's Debate Over Gay Equality.* New York: Basic Books, 2004.

Jean Lau Chin, ed.

*The Psychology of Prejudice and Discrimination.* Westport, CT: Praeger Publishers, 2004.

Faye J. Crosby

*Affirmative Action Is Dead: Long Live Affirmative Action.* New Haven: Yale University Press, 2004.

Aladdin Elaasar

*Silent Victims: The Plight of Arab & Muslim Americans in Post 9/11 America.* Bloomington, IN: AuthorHouse, 2004.

Warren Farrell

*Why Men Earn More: The Startling Truth Behind the Pay Gap—and What Women Can Do About It.* New York: AMACOM, 2005.

Steven Farron     *The Affirmative Action Hoax: Diversity, the Importance of Character and Other Lies.* Santa Ana, CA: Seven Locks Press, 2005.

David M. P. Freund     *Colored Property: State Policy and White Racial Politics in Suburban America.* Chicago: Chicago University Press, 2007.

Marci A. Hamilton     *God vs. the Gavel: Religion and the Rule of Law.* New York: Cambridge University Press, 2005.

Lingxin Hao     *Color Lines, Country Lines: Race, Immigration, and Wealth Stratification in America.* New York: Russell Sage Foundation, 2007.

Ira Katznelson     *When Affirmative Action Was White: An Untold History of Racial Inequality in Twentieth-Century America.* New York: W. W. Norton, 2005.

Mark R. Killenbeck     *Affirmative Action and Diversity: The Beginning of the End? Or the End of the Beginning?* Princeton, NJ: Educational Testing Service, 2004.

Catharine A. MacKinnon     *Women's Lives, Men's Laws.* Cambridge, MA: Belknap Press of Harvard University Press, 2005.

Michelle Malkin     *In Defense of Internment: The Case for 'Racial Profiling' in World War II and the War on Terror.* Washington, DC: Regnery, 2004.

Meridith Maran and Angela Watrous, eds.

*50 Ways to Support Lesbian & Gay Equality.* Makawao, Maui, HI: Inner Ocean Publishing, 2005.

Douglas S. Massey

*Categorically Unequal: The American Stratification System.* New York: Russell Sage Foundation, 2007.

Stephen J. McNamee and Robert K. Miller, Jr.

*The Meritocracy Myth.* Lanham, MD: Rowman & Littlefield, 2004.

Walter Benn Michaels

*The Trouble with Diversity.* New York: Metropolitan Books, 2006.

Ronald Mincy, ed.

*Black Males Left Behind.* Washington, DC: Urban Institute Press, 2006.

Evelyn F. Murphy with E. J. Graff

*Getting Even: Why Women Don't Get Paid Like Men—and What to Do about it.* New York: Simon & Schuster, 2005.

Charles J. Ogletree

*All Deliberate Speed: Reflections on the First Half-Century of Brown v. Board of Education.* New York: W. W. Norton, 2005.

Fred C. Pampel

*Racial Profiling.* New York: Facts On File, 2004.

William C. Rhoden

*$40 Million Slaves: The Rise, Fall, and Redemption of the Black Athlete.* New York: Crown Publishers, 2006.

David G. Savage

*The Supreme Court and Individual Rights*, 4th edition. Washington, DC: CQ Press, 2004.

| | |
|---|---|
| Alan Sears and Craig Osten | *The Homosexual Agenda: Exposing the Principal Threat to Religious Freedom Today*. Nashville, TN: Broadman & Holman, 2003. |
| Jennifer S. Simpson | *"I Have Been Waiting": Race and U.S. Higher Education*. Toronto: University of Toronto Press, 2003. |
| Thomas Sowell | *Black Rednecks and White Liberals*. San Francisco, CA: Encounter Books, 2005. |
| Greg Stohr | *A Black and White Case: How Affirmative Action Survived Its Greatest Legal Challenge*. Princeton, NJ: Bloomberg Press, 2004. |
| Welch Suggs | *A Place on the Team: The Triumph and Tragedy of Title IX*. Princeton, NJ: Princeton University Press, 2005. |
| Lu-in Wang | *Discrimination by Default: How Racism Becomes Routine*. New York: New York University Press, 2006. |
| Juan Williams | *My Soul Looks Back in Wonder: Voices of the Civil Rights Experience*. New York: AARP/Sterling, 2004. |
| Tim J. Wise | *Affirmative Action: Racial Preference in Black and White*. New York: Routledge, 2005. |